THE WARRIOR GORKHA

THE OFFICIAL BIOGRAPHY OF LT. COL. DHAN SINGH THAPA, PVC

MADHULIKA THAPA MONGA

An imprint of
Srishti Publishers & Distributors

Srishti Publishers & Distributors
A unit of AJR Publishing LLP
212A, Peacock Lane
Shahpur Jat, New Delhi – 110 049

editorial@srishtipublishers.com

First Published by Bold,
an imprint of Srishti Publishers & Distributors in 2025

10 9 8 7 6 5 4 3 2 1

This is a work of non-fiction based on the author's own experience and research. While due care has been taken by the author and publisher to verify contents at press time, any inadvertent miss shall be updated in subsequent editions. Actual names of individuals, places and institutions have been used for realistic representation. Certain events have been dramatized for a heightened reading experience.

Printed and bound in India

Foreword

The Warrior Gorkha — a definitive biography of Lt Col Dhan Singh Thapa, PVC is an emotionally moving account of the life of Lt Col Dhan Singh Thapa, PVC. It had to be so, as it is his own daughter who is the author of this biography.

It takes one through the difficult times the war hero experienced as a child and what probably made him mentally strong to show the courage he displayed during the 1962 Sino-Indian war. The author has not only brought to fore the family and the struggles as he grew up but also the passion and dedicatedness that Lt Col Dhan Singh Thapa, PVC acquired from his childhood. It is the likes of him who make the Indian Army proud and it is the likes of him who are worshipped by soldiers they command.

The book also brings out the 1962 war and how the Indian Army handled it on ground. It was the leaders like Lt Col Dhan Singh Thapa and the soldiers under their command who fought in adverse conditions and yet gave a bloody nose to the attackers.

This is a must-read for anyone who wants to know about the dreams, the character and the devotion of Lt Col Dhan Singh Thapa, PVC. It is the likes of him who will always be the guiding lights of for the Nations.

—General (Dr.) V.K. Singh, PVSM, AVSM, YSM
24th Chief of the Army Staff of the Indian Army

Contents

A Note From the Author

'Some people don't believe in heroes, but they haven't met my dad,' a popular quote goes.

This holds true for my dad. And I guess for most dads.

Writing this book was a huge challenge for me. I needed to capture all the nuances of his life. I had to do a lot of research, read and re-read all my father's files, and gather all the data that had been collected. A lot of Googling also connected me with people whom he had met during different periods of his life. (I connected with quite a few Army officers and many relatives that I had only heard of but never met.) And then there were some who guided me, and whom I'm thankful to. There were many stories about his life that he told us, numerous stories which my grandmother, Mrs Draupadi Thapa, narrated, and countless incidents that my mother, Mrs Shukla Thapa, keeps regaling us with. I spoke to Mr Kishan Thapa and Mr Nardev Thapa, my father's cousins, and learnt a lot about my father from them as well.

This book is my interpretation of his life.

To be honest, all the credit for this book goes to my younger sister, Poornima Thapa, who stayed with my father and looked after him till he passed away. She was the one who had collected and kept a lot of his data, including his original telegrams and the newspaper cuttings of those times. She was the one who urged us to go and meet Lt. Col. Hasabnis, who had been his roommate in the prison camps of 1962. Lt. Col. Hasabnis narrated many stories of the prison camp, which I have incorporated in the book.

The Warrior Gorkha is about my father – his childhood, his growing up years, his army days, the 1962 Indo-China war, his sojourn in the Chinese army prison camp and his return to India, his motherland.

It is a story that will inspire the youth the world over. It's a story that tells you that despite having nothing in life, you can make your country proud of you. It is about how you become the bravest of the brave. In a country with a population of more than a billion, there are only twenty-one soldiers who have been awarded the Param Vir Chakra. Fourteen were awarded posthumously, and sixteen arose from action in Indo-Pakistani conflicts.

Gratitude to my mother, Mrs Shukla Thapa; my husband, Mr Aman Monga; my daughter, Subhadra Monga; my oldest sister, Pamela Chauhan and her husband, Lt. Col. Chauhan (veteran); my brother Lt. Col. Paramdeep Thapa (veteran) and his wife Mrs Anushree Thapa, and my youngest sister Ms Poornima Thapa for encouraging me to write this book. They helped me when I would get stuck, not knowing how to move forward. Someone or the other would remind me of an incident, and my creative juices would start flowing again. I will also be forever grateful to Jona Roy who has been with me through thick and thin.

This is a humble effort on my part to document the life of a valiant man, Lt. Col. Dhan Singh Thapa.

He and our country's bravehearts are indeed the bravest of the brave.

I salute this country and I salute all those brave men and soldiers who fought for our country and coloured the soil red with their blood. I salute the widows and children who sacrificed their husbands and their fathers for our great country. I salute their amazing spirit. And also, heartfelt gratitude for their services to the nation.

These are our country's real heroes. Let's salute them and remember that every breath that we take in an independent and free India is thanks to the sacrifices of these soldiers and freedom fighters.

> *In a world full of pop heroes, fantasy heroes, and sports heroes, we should never forget to look to the real heroes for real courage, real strength and real stories.*
>
> — Steve Nethercott

Prologue

20th October 1962
4:30 a.m.
Sirijap post 1

Major Thapa had been very uneasy all night. Giving up any thoughts of sleep, he picked up his heavy jacket, pulled up his boots and decided to take a round. The blistering cold wind was rebuking him and telling him to go back to the warmth of his bunker, but his mind refused to listen.

It was a dark night with the stars glittering. He could see the mountains looming in a most sinister way as if trying to warn him of what lay ahead.

Suddenly, his eyes saw a trail of Chinese soldiers stealthily advancing towards him. Straight towards the post of Sirijap. He thought he was dreaming, seeing hundreds of Chinese soldiers making their way towards his post.

Quickly, he made his way to the guards and pointed towards the soldiers. He gestured for them to be quiet. Then he woke up Subedar Min Bahadur Gurung, and together, they woke up the rest of them. They waited till the Chinese soldiers were directly in front of them like walking ducks, and they could shoot them without much ado.

The Chinese soldiers were huge in numbers. The Indian soldiers kept shooting, and many Chinese soldiers fell, but twice as many would take their place. The Indian soldiers went on firing till the guns became too hot for them to hold. They grabbed the guns of the dead soldiers lying around them and started off again. Some unsheathed their khukris and killed the enemy soldiers with their bare hands.

There was constant shelling of artillery and mortar fire from the Chinese side, giving covering fire to the Chinese soldiers who kept moving ahead. This allowed them to reach 150 yards close to the rear of the post.

Suddenly, the artillery fire stopped. Major Thapa knew what this meant. That was the moment when hundreds of Chinese soldiers moved forward, shrieking and screaming their war cry, moving ahead with great confidence, thinking this was going to be an easy walkover. However, they underestimated the strength and resilience of the Indian soldiers. They were confronted with the wrath of the dauntless Gorkhas.

"Jai Maa Kaali Ayo Gorkhali!" screamed the Gorkhas, the war cry echoing and freezing the Chinese soldiers for a brief moment.

There was an incessant sound of firing from both sides, shattering the silence of that seemingly peaceful night. The Chinese could not fathom what the Gorkha soldiers were made of. The strength of the Great Himalayas, these mighty mountains, was seeped into their blood.

Encouraging his soldiers, running from bunker to bunker, with bullets grazing past his shoulders, Major Thapa's adrenaline soared. There was no other thought in his mind except to save his soldiers, his country and his countrymen from the Chinese assault.

These soldiers wanted to protect every inch of their country. They descended on the Chinese like the cyclone wind; their fury unleashed, destroying anything and everything that came their way. They suffered huge losses, but it was like they were on fire. They were unstoppable.

Before the communication links of the company and the battalion were destroyed, Major Thapa could be heard by the Signal Battalion saying, "Don't worry, sir. I will defend my post... I will defend my country till my last breath!"

The last message was heard by Major Ved Vyas from the Signals Regiment. Major Thapa declared valiantly, "Neither will I withdraw, nor will I surrender."

Chapter 1

FOOTBALL

The more difficult the victory, the greater the happiness in winning.

"*Jai Maha Kali, Aayo Gorkhali!*" shouted thirteen-year-old Dhan Singh. His face gleamed with perspiration and glowed red in the sunlight as his stout little body pulsed with energy. He swung the ball high with his foot, making the ball touch the skies, almost but not quite. Little did he know then that this war cry would lead him to get the highest gallantry award in the Indian Army many years later.

Dhan Singh was born in Shimla on 10th April 1928 to Prem Singh Thapa and Draupadi Thapa. He was the oldest of five siblings. He was brought up in Shimla and Solan. He and his siblings studied in Shimla, so the weekdays were spent there, while the weekends were spent in a small village called Galhut and another village called Bajrog in Solan. They had lived in Galhut village to begin with, but later, his parents bought some land in Bajrog in Solan and shifted there. The land and the house in Bajrog were looked after by a man from Nepal, whom the kids called *Jhetoba* (elder brother of the father).

When Dhan Singh was nine years old, his father walked out on his mother. They were left at the mercy of her relatives. But his mother was a brave woman who faced life like a tigress. She shifted her mother in with her and sent her two youngest sons, Kishan and Bikram, to Shimla to live with her brother.

Dhan Singh and Manu, the two older brothers, were admitted to a hostel at a Gorkha School in Summer Hill, Shimla. They had a huge joint family in Shimla with his Mamaji, his wife and their five children. His mother had five sisters. Two of those sisters were widows. And they had children as well, so between all of them, there were nine children! All nine children lived with Mamaji.

Times were tough, and the hunger gripes in the stomach were very real.

Years would pass before they got any new clothes to wear, and they understood the language of hunger very well. Despite their hardships, they had a lot of fun growing up together. So many children together were sure to cause a lot of chaos wherever they went.

Mamaji worked in the Shimla municipality and was the secretary of the Gorkha School. He was the one who suggested that two of the older children, Dhanu and Manu, be put in the hostel. He was a mild-tempered man and tried to be a strict disciplinarian. He was greatly respected for his discipline and his truthfulness.

Uncle was so honest and simple that there were numerous stories about him. One goes about how he had opened a store after retiring from his government job, but he wouldn't let his customers buy anything that was a little old or expired. In those days, there were no expiration dates for items, so people bought really old stuff without realizing that it was unfit for consumption or use. He would tell his customers, "Please don't buy this; it is very old." Naturally, he had to shut the shop down.

He tried to look after the families of his three sisters, along with his own huge family. Since his own resources were limited, he had to try very hard to take care of everyone. He decided to put two of his sister's children in the Gorkha School, and the rest of the children stayed at his home in Shimla. He tried his best. The government job did not pay too well, but at least there was a steady income coming in.

The Gorkha School was a school for orphans and children from financially weaker families. There were no fees to be paid, and the books and clothes were provided by the school. These were given to them by different Gorkha associations. So Dhanu with his brother Manu, were enrolled in this school where they learnt a lot. More than anything, they learnt to survive.

Dhanu had stood outside the school gates and had looked at his mother imploringly, "Do we have to do this?"

He refused to let go of the *pallu* of his mother's saree.

His mother hugged him gently and said, "You are the oldest, Dhanu, and you have to look after everyone – your brothers, your sister and me. How will you do this? Only by educating yourself and by becoming something or someone in life. Now, we are your responsibility, so go on and achieve something!"

He had clung to her and refused to let her go. She had held him away from her, given him one tight slap impulsively and said, "We cannot depend on your uncle all our life. He has too many people to look after."

He had run off and hidden in his dormitory, refusing to get out of bed for lunch or dinner. At dinner time, his hostel warden came to him and shook him like a rat. Looking at him with stern eyes, he told him, "If you don't come to the dining room for dinner in five minutes, no food for a whole week!"

Dhanu realized that protesting on an empty stomach was no fun. He knew what hunger meant, and he knew that hunger definitely did not understand emotions. Quickly putting his feet into his sandals, he ran to the dining room much before the five minutes were over.

He was quite upset that he had been admitted to this school. But as time went by, he understood that if he had to help his family, he had to be educated. Education was a powerful tool, and this was the only way. On the first day in school, Manu had cried incessantly. He just would not stop. Dhanu, who was quite young himself, was helpless. He did what his mother had done – gave Manu one slap and repeated what his mother had told him,

"This is the only way to do something in our life. We cannot depend on our uncle. He has too many people to look after."

Memories of those early painful days stayed in Dhanu's heart and mind for a long time.

He was an avid student, not brilliant in his studies, but a conscientious one. His passion, however, was football. He loved the sport. He played football even while he was in the Army. But he had to stop when he came back from China. He had suffered from frostbite in China after the Chinese had made him walk over the snow-clad mountains with the radio equipment on his back, barefoot. His feet used to swell up and would remain swollen for a long time, making it impossible for him to play.

As a young boy, once he was on the football field, he had no other thought in his mind but the game. Like lightning, he was here one minute and at the other end of the field the next. His mind focused on the goal his team needed. Squinting his eyes against the bright sunlight, he raced towards the goal with the ball and kicked it hard, hoping to score a goai. And when he did, he screamed, "*Jai Maha Kaali, Aayo Gorkhali!*"

This rallying battle cry of the Gorkha Regiment salutes Maha kaali as the fierce Hindu Goddess associated with universal power and life, time and death. *Aayo Gorkhali* warns the enemy that the Gorkhas are here.

Like the wind, he was all over the field, brilliant and energetic. Even later in life, he was always full of energy. Nothing was too much for him or too little.

Onlookers applauded the star as he whizzed past his opponents with the ball firmly under his control. His opponents tried unsuccessfully to take the ball from him. One fell, while another was left far behind, and the third almost managed to get it but did not.

Dhan Singh unleashed an attack on his opponents, baring his teeth, the saliva dripping from his mouth, and the sweat-soaked clothes clinging to his body. Like a ball of energy, he whirled past them with clenched hands and lightning feet. He stopped only after his team scored the winning goal. He triumphantly screamed and rolled on the ground with his teammates and then joyously jumped into his mother's arms. His teammates charged excitedly behind him, laughing victoriously, hugging him, pummeling him, and lifting him high into the air.

His brothers came charging next, cheering him on and taking turns lifting him high in the air excitedly, "Well done, *Daaji!*" He jumped to the ground from his brothers' shoulders and touched his mother's feet before hugging her.

It was a poignant moment. A thirteen-year-old victorious boy breathing shallowly, hugging her like an adult, yet looking up at her for her approval like a little child. This was a common occurrence in his childhood. He'd behave like an adult but would always yearn for approval like a little child.

His mother, Draupadi, was a thirty-five-year-old, extremely confident woman who had lived life on her own terms as her husband had left her when the children had been very young.

Draupadi lived with her mother, her daughter Shakuntala, and her two sisters in a village called Bajrog close to Solan in Himachal Pradesh. She was a courageous woman living in a rather deserted village where there were a few Gorkha families.

The Gorkhas who were settled in India liked to call themselves Gorkhalis. The Gorkhas led by Amar Singh Thapa in the year 1809 AD had captured Solan, but in 1815, it was won by the British from the Gorkhas. Gorkha Fort or Arki Fort is still standing in Solan. In fact, the British officers were so impressed by the bravery and courage shown by the Gorkha soldiers in this war that Major General David Ochterlony from the British army proposed that the Gorkha soldiers, whosoever wished so, could join the British Army.

Not only the British but also the Indian rajas and maharajas were very impressed by the valour of the Gorkhas.

The rulers of Himachal Pradesh asked Amar Singh Thapa, the General of the Gorkha Army, to fight their wars. He made good use of this opportunity and ruled the hills of Himachal Pradesh and Uttarakhand. The Gorkha kingdom of Nepal had won Kumaon Hills by 1791 and annexed Garhwal by 1804. It was also controlling Himachal on invitation by their rulers.

A lot of Gorkhas stayed back in the Himachal and Kumaon districts. A small number joined the British army as well. Some Gorkhas had made their way to Shimla and Solan. Bajrog also became home to Gorkha families who had settled there and made their living by farming in the fields.

Solan was always known as the city of red gold because of the number of tomatoes that were grown there. In Bajrog and Galhut, apart from tomatoes, farmers grew corn, maize, cauliflower, cabbage, and peas. Draupadi also grew corn and maize on her farm. She made sure that they could fend for themselves as far as food was concerned. She was one feisty lady. And strong mothers raise strong children.

This small village was very scenic, and nestled cozily in the Shivalik Hills of the Himalayas. It was surrounded by thickly wooded areas. And this is where Dhan Singh and his siblings grew up with their mother. A lot of their time was spent in Shimla with their maternal uncle, Shamsher Thapa, as well. She wanted to educate the children, but there were no schools in Solan.

Shimla, on the other hand, had many schools as it was the summer capital of the British. The British had ensured that Shimla progressed. Initially, to reach Shimla, the only mode of transportation was a bullock cart, which was dangerous in the treacherous mountainous terrain. So in 1903, the Kalka-Shimla narrow gauge was started and was referred to as the 'British jewel of the Orient'. This train allowed passengers to see the beautiful sights and the picturesque villages of Himachal Pradesh. The highlight of the journey was the Barog station, which has the longest tunnel, stretching 1,143.61 metres.

Their mother looked after the farm in Solan, employing a person to work in the fields for her. Though the boys lived away from her, they helped her with the housework and with the farming whenever they visited her. Dhan Singh, too, came down to Solan during the weekends and helped his mother in the fields.

Draupadi was a fearless lady living with her mother in a place like Bajrog. She lived in the wilderness as the next house was more than a mile away. The village was surrounded by thick, dark woods. There was no electricity, so they burnt oil lamps in the village. After sunset, the whole village would be shrouded in complete darkness.

Wild animals would come close and howl, but nothing scared this determined young woman. Solan was known for Himalayan black bears, panthers, jackals and wild cats. She would often tell funny stories about these animals to her children and later to her grandchildren.

She was a dauntless woman, not that she had an option. Sometimes in life, the lack of choices gives birth to traits in your character you never knew existed within you.

Dhan Singh got his bravest of braves attitude from her.

Draupadi was a domineering woman with a ram-rod straight body, a slightly darkish complexion, with her long straight hair tied in a plait. She had not let the circumstances of her life get her down. She took each day as it came, not worrying about the future, and she had no regrets. She was lucky to have a strong support system. There were many relatives and all of them rallied around each other. They would come to the aid of anyone who had a problem.

Though Draupadi lived with her mother, sometimes her daughter would be there with her, the fact that her brother had her back increased her confidence ten times over. An epitome of strength and grace, she had a certain aura about her. Her friends, neighbours, and relatives in Solan would come from far and near to take her advice regarding all matters. She was clearly a people person, always there for the neighbours, family, and friends – listening to them, talking to them, and helping them. She enjoyed it, and she enjoyed her life in spite of all the hardships.

That particular day, she was going to watch Dhan Singh play in a football match. The walk to the school was a long one. She walked miles from her house in Solan to her brother's house and then proceeded to the school to watch her beloved son's match. Watching her son become the hero of the match was worth the great distance she had walked.

Dhan Singh's class teacher, Diwan Singh Sir, came to meet his mother after the match and said, "Thapa is good. He has team spirit. He loves football and is very passionate about it."

Draupadi felt great pride in her son. She nodded and acknowledged his compliments. Joining both her hands, she thanked him and said, "All you teachers have made him what he is. There is a reflection of all you gurus in my son."

Seeing Dhanu run towards her, she quickly walked towards him and hugged him. She lovingly congratulated him, "You are quite good, you know."

Dhan Singh glowed in the warmth of his mother's praise and affection.

He hugged her back and said, "Your blessings make me the best footballer instead of just a good footballer."

After his father left them, Dhan Singh grew up overnight. He had matured, become responsible, and assumed the mantle of a little dad for his siblings. He felt happy that his teacher had specially come to meet his mother. His class teacher, with his Gandhian glasses, was fond of Dhanu. He worked hard at his studies and made special efforts to do better than his best.

Not that he was not naughty; he would play pranks with other kids, but was careful that the pranks never hurt or harmed anybody.

Diwan Sir, who was standing close by, smiled and said, "He is a good footballer and should be given a chance to train professionally."

"We will see," replied his mother tautly.

"I could train him, but his schoolwork could suffer a bit," offered the teacher.

Draupadi vehemently opined, "No, no, I cannot let that happen. He has to study. His first priority is studies, and then football if he can manage."

The teacher simply said, "Okay, but think about it and let me know."

Having offered his advice, he left.

Dhanu and his siblings wanted to eat the sweets sold outside the school. They wanted to celebrate Dhanu's victory, and the multi-coloured sweets attracted them like flies. They stood there stuck, refusing to budge even after their mother scolded them.

Dhanu watched them from the corner of his eyes. His siblings beseeched for a treat. But he knew that his mother would never allow them to have the sweets. He knew she could not really afford them as every penny was saved for their education and upbringing. She spent sparingly. She had to, and the children knew that, so they never made a fuss. But once in a while, they felt tempted.

Dhan Singh did not want to embarrass her, neither did he want to get embarrassed because she was quite capable of bashing the whole lot of them in front of his teammates, so he ran away, saying, "Race you and the last one to come is a donkey."

Forgetting the sweets, the boys ran after him as did his sister. None of them wanted to be the last one. And soon the kids were running up and down the slopes with the cold wind cooling their warm, flushed faces. The school was soon out of sight. They sat down on the side benches waiting for their mother to join them.

A while later, they spotted her walking towards them. To Dhanu's surprise, she was holding a packet of sweets.

"Had to celebrate your goals," she laughingly said as she distributed the sweets.

Chapter 2

School

> Let us remember one book one pen,one child and one teacher can change the world.
>
> — Malala Yousafzai

Dhan Singh soon turned fifteen. As he grew more mature, he felt more comfortable to deal with whatever life threw his way. His brothers were also grown up, and they helped on the farm. Life, in general, had comparatively become more comfortable for the family.

Life at the Gorkha School had been a new experience for him and his brother. He had learnt a lot in this school. It had been his mother's dream to educate her sons and she could not afford any better. So, when her brother suggested Gorkha boarding school as this school offered free scholarship and free boarding, she jumped at it.

It was tough at the outset. It had been so difficult that Manu used to cry every day. Dhanu, too, would want to sit and cry, but then, who would look after Manu? The two of them would hug each other and try to be brave.

The worst times were the meal times when they were served watery dal and rice. They sat on the mat placed on the cold floor. The only good thing about this meal was that it was served piping hot, and it helped keep them warm. Whatever it was, it filled their bellies, and they would not get hunger gripes at night.

Sometimes, they got lucky. People would donate a meal and get some vegetables with their dal and chawal. On rare occasions, they got a mithai with their meal, thanks to the kindness of some local people who wanted to help out. They would come once or twice and sometimes even thrice a month with some good food and sweetmeats.

It was with a good feeling that he woke up that morning. When he went out to the dining area, he could see some well-dressed people outside. This couple came quite often to their school to donate food. This meant that they would get good food that day. People often came to the school to celebrate birthdays or any other occasion, and would donate food or sweetmeats, clothes or books for the children.

These were the days the children looked forward to. These were the days when the children ate to their heart's content and enjoyed their special meal.

Dhanu learnt the value of food in school when he was growing up. As a result, later in life too, he never wasted food. He always finished what was on his plate. This school had a good system in place. Everyone had their own plates and glasses, which each child washed and kept with him or herself. If a student lost his plate, there would be no food for him. But having learnt survival tricks, the children managed to share the food so that no one went hungry.

Everything in the school was controlled by the cane. The teachers caned you for the tiniest mistake; the hostel superintendent caned you if you disobeyed him; the cane was the punishment for everything. The school was full of rules and regulations as they felt it was the only way to control and teach the street urchins, orphans and poor children. The cane would come down swishing if you made mistakes. All the children dreaded the cane, but this cane was magical as it disciplined the children.

On days like this, when all the children were fed properly and after they had eaten good food, there was a cheerful atmosphere all around. The warm sunlight blazing into the classrooms would make some of them sleepy and they would creep under their tables and sleep till their teachers found them, quickly followed by the swishing cane.

That day, after the morning meal, Dhanu rushed to his class to sit in his usual seat which was right in the front. His poker straight hair was well-oiled. He tried to flatten it, which was almost impossible. He managed to make half of it flat while the rest stood up straight. There was an earnestness about him which attracted people to him.

The family that had come to donate food would come to meet the children. The mother always came and hugged him. He loved the attention, though it made the other children quite jealous. From the very beginning, there was a certain spark in little Dhanu.

"How are you, Dhanu?" the lady would ask.

Very shyly, he would nod his head and say, "I am okay!"

Diwakar Sir would tell the lady, "He is a very good footballer. He will be a great man one day."

Dhanu would go red in his face, embarrassed but humbled at all the attention he was receiving.

The school hostel had strict rules and regulations, and the teachers made sure they were implemented. Everyone in the hostel had to get up early and take a cold-water wash, and then they would wash their own clothes. They would proceed for the morning assembly and prayers, followed by breakfast. They also had to help with some of the hostel chores. Everyone had to take turns cleaning the hostel and also help in the kitchen. It was all done in rotation so that nobody missed their classes.

Though a conscientious student, Dhanu had his moments of naughtiness. He would bunk school whenever there was a football match in town. And whenever he was unfortunate to be caught, he would be beaten black and blue. But for Dhanu, it was worth it. His passion for football was so great that he never minded the caning. Manu, on the other hand, bunked school all the time and would loaf around all over Shimla. He was also quite used to the caning. For a few days, he would attend classes quite regularly after a vicious caning session but then would soon go back to his old ways.

One thing Dhanu could not bear was injustice of any kind. He hated it when his hostel teachers would take out their anger on the younger children and beat them for no rhyme or reason. One day, seeing a small child being caned, Dhanu lost it. He took the cane and broke it into pieces. So great was his anger that he remained trembling with fury. He would have been expelled, but he was spared as his uncle was the secretary of the school. But after that, he got a reputation of sorts, and teachers would not take any undue advantage of him.

However, his mother came to the school and gave him a caning he would remember all his life. Then she took him for a walk and explained to him that as he was the oldest son, he had to take care of everyone. If he had been thrown out of this school, his education would not have been completed, as there was no other school she could afford. So, he had to behave himself and learn to control his temper. There would be no next time, she explained to him with tears in her eyes. His uncle had a tough time pleading with everyone of importance in that school to let him stay.

He nodded sheepishly. He couldn't bear to see the tears in her eyes, and he too started to cry, "No, no! I will never do it again. I love you Ma, please, please don't cry. I promise you this will never happen again!"

All her life, she had gone through a lot of hardships, but he had never seen her cry. But that day, when he saw the tears in her eyes, he realized the enormity of his actions. He understood the importance of education and also the fact that he had to take care of his mother and his siblings. This had been an important lesson in his life. He swallowed hard and hugged his mother tightly, telling her he would never misbehave again. She hugged him back. She missed her boys a lot. Whenever she came up to Shimla, she would walk down to the school to watch Dhanu play football or just go and sit with him.

Dhan Singh was getting older and was quite used to the hostel and the hardships of the school. But he had learnt a lot during these experiences. These hardships eventually became blessings in his life when he had to face life and death situations. He always had a positive aura about him and survival instincts ingrained ever since his childhood. He did not have much negativity, or it was the situation that he grew up in that did not allow him the luxury of negativity.

***

On a particular day, tossing and turning on his narrow bed, Dhan Singh was in no mood to get up. He had come down to the village for the weekend, and he was enjoying the comfort of home. The previous day, he had played football, and the match had been hectic, tiring him out completely. He just wanted to sleep for another hour. He loved his sleep, but then he shook the sleep away. He told himself another half an hour, and then he'd get up, and he did. There was a lot of work planned for the day. They say sleeping is hard when you can't stop thinking, but for Dhan Singh, nothing disturbed his sleep. And his mind was forever ticking – thinking and planning – though his body remained fast asleep. Later in life, in the Army, he could strangely even stand and sleep. He had trained himself to do that. Dhan Singh's mind was always full of thoughts, but he still slept on to give the body adequate rest. He had to have a talk with his mother regarding his brothers and sister, since he was the eldest and the responsibility of his mother and siblings rested on his shoulders. He would definitely take care of his family, and this was taken for granted by him and his family. Suddenly full of energy, he started whistling and went into the kitchen. He took a glass of milk gulped it down, and then went looking for his mother. She must be in the fields, he thought, wiping his mouth with the back of his hand. He went out to the fields, and sure enough, she was there, guiding the labour.

"Why didn't you wake me up?'

"I knew that as soon as you get up, you'd make your way here!" his mother replied.

"I have to get a sack of vegetables ready to take to Shimla for uncle."

"Take corn this week. We've already harvested it."

Dhan Singh nodded his head.

He started to work in the fields with the labourers, laughing and joking with them. Soon, he had the job pretty much under control. His mother went back home as she had to make lunch for the two of them. Dhan Singh wanted to talk to her, so she wanted to take out some time for him.

In the afternoon, Dhan Singh came back home. After a great wholesome lunch of dal chawal, his favourite now, and some *saag*, he lay down for some time.

Then, calling out for his mother, he told her, "You better talk to your sons Manu, Bikram and Kishan. They don't attend school, and when they do, they don't want to concentrate on their studies. When they come here, they do not want to work in the fields. Last time, they said they were not labourers, so why should they work in the fields? That was their attitude."

His mother grimaced. The younger boys were quite uncontrollable, but Dhan Singh managed them well. There were times he got quite fed up though. After all, he was only fifteen.

Their life was full of frustrations and hardships, but according to Dhanu, they shouldn't ever let the circumstances get them down. In fact, he told them to treat the challenges as lessons to face bigger obstacles in life. The brothers were young, no doubt, but they had to be shown the right way.

Draupadi was in the village of Solan most of the time, so there was no strong hand to control the younger boys. She was forever reprimanding them, but then there was no one else they would listen to. And frankly speaking, they didn't want to. For the children, there were always too many distractions that made them stray from their path. There was a marble gang, and they were an inherent part of it. She had found many marbles in their pockets, so she knew why they were bunking school. She needed to have a serious talk with them.

"I am going to have a talk with them," she said.

"I think you need to; otherwise, their studies will suffer."

"What I need to do is come and spend more time in Shimla till my children are on the right track."

Dhan Singh nodded, "That seems like a good idea."

"So, it is settled then?"

Having settled the matter, he went back to the fields.

In Dhanu, Draupadi saw a fifteen-year-old boy with a glint in his eyes and determination in his walk. She was very proud of him.

He always fulfilled his responsibilities and never spoke of his worries to anybody. He made the best of what life had given him. This habit of not talking to anybody about his problems stayed with him all his life. He never spoke to anybody about his worries or his difficulties. But he worried a lot, and that was a problem. His head was always full of plans and ideas. And that's all he had – dreams, hope and faith.

His mother tried to placate him, "I will make sure they go to the farm with you and that they also attend school. This time, I will make sure."

Dhan Singh nodded his head, as all of this had been discussed before, but to no avail.

They were the best brothers one could have, ever ready to do anything for him, but as far as they themselves were concerned, they just wouldn't listen. They were a scruffy lot. With no father to control them, they ran wild.

Dhan Singh tried hard, but he wasn't the father, which is something he heard from them more than once. Once, he and Manu had a furious fight, and they almost killed each other. It began with a small bottle which Manu had found. He had filled it with water, and he was troubling everyone with that. He would shout, "*Holi hai bhai Holi!*" getting on everyone's nerves. Dhanu walked up to him and asked him for the bottle, but Manu refused to give it to him. Then, they started a huge fight, with Dhanu hitting him and Manu retaliating by scratching him. It was ferocious. Manu was giving back as well as he was getting, but Dhanu truly thrashed him that day.

Shakuntala went screaming to her mother, "Ma, please stop them; they are killing each other!"

Draupadi dragged both of them away from each other, shouting, "Stop it! I say stop it."

Dhanu explained, "Ma, he is troubling everyone, so I was trying to stop him!"

Manu cried, "You are my brother; stop trying to be my father!"

That was a big lesson for Dhanu. He realized that he could take care of them as a big brother; he did not have to get into his father's shoes to do the same. Every day was a day of new learning for him. He learnt to be independent from a very early age.

So independent was he that on most Monday mornings, he made sure a sack of vegetables arrived at his uncle's house from their farm. He did not want to feel obliged to anyone. The fact that his two brothers lived with his uncle irked him, but there was no other way out. The Gorkha school denied admission to any more of the brothers so their uncle's abode was the only place they could stay at.

It was therefore imperative that they should return their kindness and the only way was to gift them some of the farm's products. Sometimes it was corn, other times maize or fruits or vegetables. He wanted to be indebted to no one. People like him were different, even as children. He made sure that on most Monday mornings, he arrived in Shimla with his offerings. Obligations had to be returned.

***

It was Monday morning, and he had to be in Shimla. Having walked two kilometres from his house to the bus stop with the sack of corn on his back, he was huffing and puffing. It was a cold day, and the sack weighed a ton. His precious canvas shoes, which he tried to preserve for football, were on their way out. They did nothing to keep the cold out of his feet, but he needed them to play football, so he took good care of them. It was bitterly cold, so he had to wear his invaluable pair of shoes; otherwise, he would have worn his rubber chappals.

He was so concerned that nothing should happen to his shoes that whenever he stopped to rest, he would look down to see if the shoes were okay.

The harsh, cold wind hit him on his face. After walking a kilometre, he put the sack down and rubbed his hands. They felt raw, and the cold did nothing to help, but then he had to keep moving. After a brief rest, he picked up his sack and started again. It was a dark morning, but he knew the trail well. Another kilometre, and he stopped again. These challenges that he faced in childhood later moulded him into the person that he became in life.

He reached the bus stop as the sky had changed its colour from dark purple to a lighter shade. He quickly got on, putting the sack on top of the bus. The bus had its headlights on in the dark morning as the passengers made themselves comfortable. They were ready to take a small nap before they reached their destinations.

Dhanu chose the seats in the last row, lay down and promptly went off to sleep. He generally walked up to Shimla from Solan, but not on Monday mornings. He preferred to take the bus, especially if he was alone with a sack full of vegetables. But if his brothers were there, they would take turns carrying the sack and would walk to Shimla together.

That morning, he was looking forward to the bus ride as he would get that extra hour of sleep. He was an expert at this – falling asleep anywhere and everywhere. The bus stopped at half a dozen villages before it finally reached Shimla. It had been a long weekend in the village. He had worked hard in the fields as they had harvested the corn. His brothers had not come to the village, so Dhanu had worked alone in the fields with some labourers. When he reached Shimla, his brothers helped him to take the sack back home.

He constantly worried about his little brothers. One day, he had come to his Mamaji's house during lunch time and his youngest brother Bikram was having his lunch. His plate had only a chapatti, some salt and one raw onion. This really upset him. At least Manu and he got rice and hot dal in the hostel. He had never forgotten that scene all his life.

His heart had literally wept, but he could do nothing. He just held Bikram close and hugged him. Bikram wondered what was wrong with Daaji. He was hungry and wanted to finish his food, and Daaji was getting emotional instead. Dhanu turned red in his face, his eyes turned all teary. He wanted to throw away that bare plate, but he knew if he did that, Bikram's meal for the day would be gone. So, he controlled himself and let Bikram finish his meal.

His aunt shouted from the kitchen, "Dhanu, do you want to eat something?"

Looking at Bikram's food, he shouted back, "No, I am going back to the hostel. I will eat there."

All the children instinctively hated being dependent on their uncle and aunt. Losing their father had left them with a sense of great insecurity. Both Mama and Mami were good people, but they both had their constraints. Mama had financial restrictions, and Mami had many children of her own. She literally went berserk trying to take care of so many children. But they were good people, and they tried their best. She made sure all the children were fed. She was very clear about one thing, though. First, she took care of her own children and fed them, and then the other children would get the leftovers. She made sure they were fed, even if it was just raw onions and chapatis at times. Physically, she was a big woman, so the children were automatically scared of her. Not only the children but even Mama was scared. Luckily, Mami and Draupadi got on fabulously well. They had their own private conversations. They would bicker and laugh and could spend hours together. All this was fine, but Draupadi's five children were always the extra five. The extra ones.

Nobody said anything to make them feel that they were extra, but it was an automatically felt emotion. It was not easy, but they learnt to live with it. Being together helped smoothen the rough edges. They became sort of rebels against the world, deeming themselves to be the victims of fate. However, Dhanu didn't think so, as his mind was occupied with planning his next move to ensure the smooth running of his household. He really had no time for this emotional frivolity. He and his mother understood this feeling of unwanted dependency but could do very little about it.

Draupadi was very grateful to her brother for taking care of her five children, besides so many of his own. Her brother was a simple man who lived with his own set of problems. He admired Dhanu and his protectiveness towards his family, especially towards his mother and sister. Dhanu never forgot his Mama's kindness. When he started working, he would always send money to his uncle. He knew his uncle had taken care of his family despite all odds. He was always there for this family, and the family was always grateful and held him in great regard throughout his life.

Most weekends were full of fun. The two younger brothers would run wild after finishing all the chores. The other two from the Gorkha school were not allowed home every weekend, but when they got a little older, the restrictions eased. The brothers would walk from Shimla to Solan. They knew all the shortcuts and would be in Solan in no time. They would start from their Summer Hill hostel at ten in the morning after the morning meal and begin their long walk. They'd reach Solan by late afternoon, get to the fields if there was work to be done, or just laze around at home and go to the fields early the next morning. But work excited Dhanu, so invariably, he ended up going to the fields after resting for a while and having his cup of tea. Draupadi would shout after him, "Leave it, Dhanu, tomorrow is another day!"

"I will be back in an hour's time," Dhanu would shout, rushing to reach the fields before it got dark.

"Let him be, Ma," said Manu, who was lolling around sipping his tea. "You know Daaji, he has a hundred plans in his mind. He won't rest till he goes to the field and sees what's to be done and how it is to be done."

They would walk back to Shimla in the dark through the jungles and take shortcuts so that they could stay at home for a while longer. They feared nothing and no one, so the seeds of fearlessness were sown very early in the boys.

Weekends were generally spent with their mother, and weekdays were spent at school in Shimla. It was strange how there was so much to do all the time. They got up early, finished the chores at school, and then off they went for their classes. This was followed by football and time with friends. It did not end there. Once they were back in the hostel, they had to complete the chores again, finish their homework, and finally sleep amidst a lot of noise.

Meal times were great fun, with all the children sitting in a line on the floor, gulping down piping hot dal and chawal. Dhanu invariably burned his tongue as he would put the first morsel of dal and chawal in his mouth without even waiting for it to cool down. The sweet bantering between all of them was always the highlight of the meal. Nobody dared to fight during meal times, as the minute a fight broke out between any two, the rest of the children would gobble up the food on the plates of the children fighting. And once your share of the food was gone, there was simply no more. So, no one dared to fight during meal times for fear of going hungry till the next meal came along.

Bedtime was great fun too, with someone grabbing the quilt, and another grabbing the pillows. The boys put the mattresses on the floor and there would be a lot of good-natured fighting over pillows and mattresses. And other times, it would turn into a serious fight and then it was like hell had been set free with little and big bodies hitting each other, a lot of shouting, whooping and screaming. But the children were scared of waking Dhanu up as sleep was a dear thing for him. He would usually be fast asleep in the midst of the chaos.

The fear of waking him up and getting thrashed with whatever he could lay his hands on petrified them. So just one shout from him "*Go to sleep all of you!*" would send the kids scurrying to their beds.

CHAPTER 3

SIBLINGS

> Power, that's one thing, but love of family and of siblings is more important, is more powerful than any other power – at least earthly power, at least earthly power.
>
> — Sander Levin

Manu, Bikram, Kishan, and Shakuntala were good-looking kids. They were tall and slim and each one of them had an attitude. Shakuntala, being the only sister, was adored by the brothers. Despite all the hardships, they had a lot of fun together. There was a lot of good-natured teasing among them. However, they all listened to Dhanu. And especially after the last fight with Manu, he had earned their respect. His was the last word in any argument. Being the oldest, the mantle of responsibility of the siblings fell on him after his father had left.

Dhanu tried to ensure that his brothers worked hard, while the brothers made sure they played hard, as it came naturally to them. As in most large families, they had much enjoyment in their lives and did not worry about the nitty-gritty of what life had to offer them. They cherished the happy and hard times equally. They were a boisterous lot. They had emotional moments which did upset them, but they put those down as life experiences or lessons.

Dhanu knew his brothers could take care of themselves. He worried only about his sister, Shakuntala. His heart broke every time he saw her working around the house. If she went to Shimla, the onus of the housework would fall on her. She would be working without a break! Their aunt would tell her to cook lunch, which was a humungous affair. She had to do the dishes and clean the house. Mami helped her, but Shakuntala did most of the work. And then she had to deal with everyone's demands. As she would go about her work solemnly, he wished he could take her away. But Solan was too isolated for a young girl, and schooling in Solan was a problem as well. She hoped he would take her away, too.

Very solemnly, she would hug him and say in an innocent voice, "Daaji, how long will it take for you to grow up?"

Dhanu would then unashamedly wipe his tears with the back of his hand and guffaw loudly and say, "Not too long now. Then, I will turn our house into a palace and you will be the princess and mother will be the queen of the palace."

"Now let me go," he would say.

Dhanu would leave with a heavy heart every time, but also with a resolution that he would soon have all his family together in the village in Solan and make his house into a home. It would be a home where they could laugh, joke, bicker or fight; a place of their own.

Dhanu was a teenager now, good-looking with a tall, slim body, eyes full of dreams and aspirations, and lips always ready to smile. Even now, all sadness forgotten, he jogged down the hill back to Summer Hill, back to school.

As he made his way back, Dhanu smiled at himself, thinking about his brothers. Like Shakuntala, they loved him and wanted to do what he asked them to do, but unlike Shakuntala, they rarely obeyed him. Shakuntala always obeyed her brother for the lack of any option and also because of the love she had for him.

Before leaving he had gently chided them, "Both of you need to attend school regularly. Yes, I know you have a lot of work here but education is a must. Both of you should get up before sunrise, finish the work here and go to school. After school, help Uncle."

Nodding their heads in a clamour of "Yes, Daaji," they followed him as always till the end of the road when he went back to school. This time, Manu had decided he would miss two or three days of school as there was work in the fields. Manu was looking forward to the break. Dhanu was returning alone to school this time. He couldn't miss school as his exams were around the corner. The younger brothers were staying back as well.

They were good kids, happy to just be, and always on the lookout for fun. They were a restless lot and completely out of control in the absence of a father figure. However, they loved their mother immensely and she was a lady of great strength. She was the only one who had any control over them. But the fact remained that she was not there most of the time, though she knew she had to keep a strict eye on them to prevent them from running astray.

They worked as hard as they could, even though fun and games pervaded their hard work. Perhaps one reason for their working hard was that their mother was famed for caning anyone and everyone. She caned first and listened later. The school was the same – the teachers caned first and listened later.

However, there was one teacher in the school who supported the kids. If there was a problem, they always went to him, and he would advise them as best he could. He was the same teacher, the one with the Gandhian glasses, who had spoken to Draupadi about Dhanu's talent as a footballer. He listened to their problems and guided them. And because of him, they enjoyed school.

In a way, the school was good for them. It made them forget their day-to-day problems, insecurities, and their everyday challenges. But once they came back from school, back to Shimla, the bleakness of perpetual gratitude grated on their nerves. And this sometimes made them rude, while at other times they became over-helpful though they strove to retain a balance.

Despite everything, they loved life and lived it to the fullest. And, as most children do, they went with the flow of life.

Chapter 4

THE LITTLE MAN

The family is one of nature's masterpieces.

After lecturing Manu for almost an hour, which he did nearly every alternate day, Dhanu raced to the football grounds. It was match day, and he loved his football matches.

He was so obsessed with the game that he used to hang his football shoes outside his classroom on a tree. And the moment the school got over, he would jump out from the classroom window. He could not even wait to leave through the door; his passion for football was so great. He would just jump from the window, untie the shoes from the tree, and sprint to the grounds.

"Dhan Singh, you are late!" mumbled his teammates.

Dhanu and his team decided that they were going to win that day, but Lady Luck decided to side with the opposing team. He had always believed that when you decide you want something really badly, you always mostly got it. But it didn't seem to be working in this case. His team was trying hard, but so was the other team. Maybe the want of the other team was greater.

The game started with neither team scoring any goals. The first few minutes flew past without any incident of sorts, with the other team seeing the majority of the ball on their side of the field. It was only after break time that the action started. Though

Dhanu was bold and adventurous, he was given a rough time, and his team became conservative in passing the ball in the game. The game had now reached a frantic pace.

It was just by chance that the ball had been passed to Dhanu, who was quite close to the goal. Dhanu saw neither left nor right; he just kicked the ball, and it went whizzing past everyone and straight into the goal. But nothing much was accomplished with that goal except that it was a saving grace because the opposite team had scored too many goals, and they had the game in their pocket. It also gave his teammates a bit of encouragement, considering everyone knew that it was a lost cause.

"Let's go get them!" screamed Dhanu.

They fought tooth and nail but lost the match despite Dhanu and the team having tried their best. He had tried to motivate the team, if not to win the game, at least to give the opposition a hard victory. There was a fresh movement in the game when his best friend Naren also hit a goal. But the opposite team was on fire. They kept scoring goals and eventually went on to win.

It was late when the game got over and he knew he was going to get a mouthful from his mother. After losing the game, he was in no mood to listen to his mother's cribbing. He was dog-tired.

But to his surprise, his mother was all smiles. She was in a good mood. She hugged the dirty, sweaty Dhanu, who was now taller than her and told him proudly, "I met your teacher today, and he seems very happy with you. He seems to think you are going to go places if you keep on studying like this."

Dhanu smiled a tired smile. He loved it when his mother was happy.

He told his mother, "Yes, mother, I will study hard and make you very proud of me." Unable to get football out of his system, he proudly shared, "Even today, I scored two goals, Mother."

Smiling, she replied, "Yes, I know. One day you will be a great man. Not only will you make me proud but you will make the country also proud. But I want a promise from you. I want you to take care of your brothers and sister, whatever happens."

Dhan Singh promised in earnestness he would. And he meant every word of that promise.

And he did all his life. He was always there for them, and so were they.

She hugged him and told him, "Now you go to sleep as it's going to be a long day tomorrow. Today has been tiring for you."

Even before she had finished saying that, he crashed. His slim, sturdy body rolled into a ball as he fell into a deep slumber. He slept without any of his constant worries niggling him. Nothing could disturb his sleep.

Lovingly, Draupadi tousled his hair. Her little man, she thought with a smile. She had come to Shimla for a few days to spend some time with the children. But between school and their everyday chores, they hardly got any time together. Yet, her presence gave them secure warmth in which they basked.

Chapter 5

Somu, Jaanu, Naanu

> No matter how little money and how few possessions you own having a dog makes you rich.
>
> — Louis Sabin

The cold, chilly winds of Shimla cooled his nose, hands and head. The icy winds of December spared no one. He was shivering, but he knew that ten minutes of brisk walking would sort that out. His warden had allowed him to go out on the condition that he would be back in time for his classes.

His teachers, by now, had become his good friends, and he was more than allowed to do what he wanted. Years of struggle in this school had now paid off; he was now an old-timer and a senior. He was going back to Solan from school that day.

Weekends were mostly spent in Solan. Dhanu was very busy that particular day. Football had taken a secondary place, as he had important things to do that day. He had to go to the market to buy seeds for his farm. Being a pleasant boy, he made friends with one and all. And at such a young age, he commanded a certain respect from them as well.

The mantle of responsibility that he carried had made him such. He was always polite and courteous, which worked for him in a place like Solan, inhabited by simple, like-minded people.

If anyone faced a problem, be it a neighbour or an uncle, it was considered the entire village's problem. And everyone got together to sort it out.

In the village, there was a great deal of admiration and goodwill for both him and his mother, who, despite everything, lacked nothing and lived a life of decorum. Dhanu was now all of fifteen. He was thin, but he had incredible strength. In both body and mind.

After school, he went to the bus stop and caught the first bus out running. He stood on the ladder attached to the back of the bus and hung on to it till he reached Solan.

Solan was about forty-four kilometres away from Shimla. It took more than two hours on a bus because the bus would stop at every village on the way. Otherwise, it didn't take longer than an hour.

It was an enjoyable ride with beautiful scenery. The road was flanked by trees on both sides, and Dhanu enjoyed the ride back and forth immensely.

He reached Solan in the evening. He had got into a bad bus which cranked all the way to Solan and stopped every five minutes. His brothers were coming down later, but he was quite sure they must have reached much before him.

On the way home, he saw three little puppies, and he fell in love with them. He had always been very fond of animals and birds. Looking at their chocolate brown eyes, his heart melted. Their mother was nowhere in sight. He tickled them a bit and cuddled them.

When he started walking home, they followed him. He was enjoying them scampering around him and following him around, but he knew they wouldn't be welcomed by his mother, so he kept trying to shoo them away. He tried scaring them away but to no avail. Eventually, they followed him till he reached home.

He knew exactly what was going to happen once he reached home. His mother would take one look at the puppies and there would be a huge commotion. Sure enough, his mother looked at the puppies who had followed him inside the house, picked them up and left them outside the door.

"That's where they belong, and that's where they are going to stay," she said sternly.

Dhanu followed the puppies out of the house and he said to his mother, "If my puppies are going to stay out of the house, so will I." And he lay down on the cold hard ground with his puppies.

"Don't behave like this. I have enough problems as it is. You've brought home puppies. God knows what your brothers are going to get next. So get up and come inside."

Dhanu refused to get up. His back was cold and hurting, and the thought of his warm cozy bed was driving him insane. So, as soon as his mother came out to call him the second time, he did not wait for the third call. He was inside the house in a jiffy. After filling his stomach with hot dal and chawal, he went to his bed and was fast asleep within minutes.

Dhanu's ideology was akin to Pearl S. Buck, who says 'a hungry man can't see right or wrong; he just sees food.'

His siblings had reached home, and one look from him ensured there were no smart jibes about the puppies. But they loved dogs too, so it was in their common interest to keep quiet about it.

It was a joyous moment for all of them to be home together. Each one had so much to talk about. Draupadi looked at them with great love. These were the moments she lived for. Shakuntala looked content and secure. She loved her brothers, and at times like this, she felt warm and loved. She had wanted to talk to Dhanu about new clothes, but she kept quiet. These were the times she relished, and she refused to spoil them with her problems.

All of them longed to wear good clothes and smart shoes, but they were resigned to the hand-me-downs they got. These cheerful times overcame all their desires, and they were more than content just being together. After an hour of chatting and laughing, they all made a beeline for their beds.

However, an hour later, he heard a scraping sound at the door. Half an hour later, they heard indignant barks. The puppies were getting angry at being left out in the cold; they, too, wanted their share of the warm bed. Realizing the imminent danger of his mother waking up and creating a ruckus, Dhanu got up and went out. He brought in the three puppies and put them under the quilt with him. Soon, there was only the sound of the collective snoring of the puppies, the brothers and Dhanu.

Before dawn broke out, in the weak light of the moon, he stepped out and let the puppies out. He fed them a bit of milk, and they joyously drank it. Soon, they were scampering all around the yard.

Chapter 6

MANU

Be happy for this moment, for this moment is your life

— Omar Khayyam

When Dhanu returned to Shimla on Monday morning, he took along three of his friends. He decided to name them Somu, Jaanu and Naanu. He put them in a basket and took them to school. Luckily, the bus driver loved dogs as well, so he didn't mind the puppies being boarded onto the bus.

Once they reached Shimla, Manu and he walked to the school with their new friends following closely. Manu tried to pick all three puppies in his arms, but somehow or the other one of them would squeeze out of his arms and fall down. Surprisingly, they always fell on their feet.

"Put them down," ordered Dhanu imperiously.

"Okay." Manu gently put them down.

Three of them wagged their tails and only wanted Dhanu, since he was the one who had brought them home and fed them, and had slept with them.

They became his three staunch followers. Soon, there was a crowd of children around the puppies, cuddling them and feeding them.

None of them paid any attention to the ringing of the school bell till the school guard landed onto them. Shooing them to their classrooms he yelled, "Everyone, go to your classrooms!"

The children scooted. Except Dhanu who looked at the guard and asked him, "Can you look after my puppies till I finish my classes?"

The guard twirled his luxuriant moustache and patted his back and told him "You go attend your class and come to the gate after your class. They will be there with me."

One problem sorted, thought Dhanu. The next was to deal with Aunty and Uncle.

He was planning to leave the puppies there. He knew he was being an optimist, but he thought there was no harm in asking. Maybe they would agree. Eventually, he did not have to ask them as the guard kept them in his quarters and fed them the hostel's leftover food.

Dhanu and Manu tried to look after them as well as they could. Later, when they became a little bigger, they took them back to the village, where they lived outside the house happily and were old enough to fend for themselves.

One day, while eating his food during lunchtime, he suddenly remembered the puppies. Tucking the rotis inside his shirt, he and Manu sped to the guard's room. The puppies, seeing Dhanu and Manu, started to create a ruckus. But they quietened when they were fed the rotis. After feeding the dogs, the brothers sat down to finish a bag full of litchis, which they had gotten for them from the farm. They had managed to hide it in the hostel. They both attacked the huge bag of litchis, and soon, their clothes, faces, and fingers were covered with the gooey, sweet, sticky juice of the litchis.

Dhanu and Manu had a good time together. They would help people with fruit-gathering, collecting apples, litchis and cherries. Getting bags of the same fruit they had helped pick, they would devour them with great joy.

Diving into the cold Shimla rivers and running around to stop the shivering after the swim was another favourite pastime. Soon it was five of them (the three puppies as well) jumping into the cold waters. Those were happy times.

CHAPTER 7

RELIGIOUS MAN

> Prayers does not change God but it changes him who prays.
>
> — Soren Kierkegaard

Life had never been easy for Dhanu, but he had a knack for making every tough task fun. He did this all through his life.

He was a tough and brave child toughened by the circumstances of life. A tough life with responsibilities did not allow him the luxury of negative characteristics. He never had the time nor the inclination to think mean thoughts, engage in petty quarrels or be dishonest. He was too busy fulfilling his responsibilities and of taking care of his siblings and his mother. He had a short temper. However the caning in the school effectively took care of it, so it remained under control.

Life had taught him to be religious. Religion was what gave him hope and what made him look forward to a future full of unimaginable joy. Draupadi, his mother, was also a religious and ritualistic woman. Every day, early in the morning, after a sweet, sugary cup of tea, she would bathe and wear one of her cotton sarees and sit in her temple and pray. Only after that would the rituals of life be allowed to commence. Dhanu followed suit. He would be up early in the morning, wearing his cotton dhoti. After a cup of tea, just like his mother and several others living in the hilly areas, he would do his puja. Only then would the day begin.

Draupadi made the most of her life in Solan and Shimla. In Solan, she would enjoy going to neighbours' houses, sitting next to a fire place, chatting and having tea and pakoras. In Shimla, she would force her sister-in-law to go for walks along the meandering roads of the beautiful hill station. Both of them would sit in the *hawa ghars* of Shimla, chatting about everything under the sun and enjoying the breeze which blew in from all sides. They would talk about their dreams and aspirations for their children or even about run-of-the-mill things like what to cook for dinner or lunch. Or they'd just sit and laugh, look at people, make comments about them and enjoy the moment.

"*Oh bhaiya, do chai dena*," Mami would call out to the little boy walking around with a kettle of hot tea. He would serve them tea in small, chipped ceramic cups.

Sipping their tea, they would enjoy their early evening and rush home before the sun went down. Simple people, simple joys.

Draupadi had a huge zest for life and would infect everyone she met with the joy of life. If nothing else, she would tramp all the way to see Dhanu's match or his practice sessions. She would take the children with her and they would have a great time, cheering, clapping and laughing, excited about the goals scored by Dhanu. They would get really upset when he would miss one.

With Dhanu she had a deep connection, which was unexplainable. He was the little man in her life. He shouldered her responsibilities with amazing ease. He was her guiding light throughout her life. Even that day, he was the one to tell her to go to Shimla.

"Yes, yes, I was planning to go this week as well. I will come with you this Monday."

"That is nice because I have a match on Monday, and I would love it if you came and watched me play. This is an important match. We lost to the DAV School last time. This time, I want to make sure that we win. Also, this weekend Bikram and the others couldn't come to Solan, so it will be nice if you come with me. You will meet the whole group."

His mother smiled and patted him. She knew when he was adamant about something, he would end up doing it. And right now, he was adamant that she come to Shimla. She hugged her little man and tousled his hair.

On Monday morning, both mother and son set off for Shimla. On reaching home, they were surrounded by all the kids, each one hugging the other. Then she turned to greet her brother, a mild man waiting patiently for his turn.

"How are you?" she asked him.

"I am fine."

"When are you coming to Solan? Your sisters and mother are missing you, and they want to see you."

Her two sisters were widows, and they sometimes came down to Solan to stay with her and her mother.

"Soon, I will come down to Solan and meet everyone," smiled Shamsher Singh.

In the evening, Draupadi and the children went to the football grounds to watch Dhanu play.

'*Chalo goal karo*' was Draupadi's favourite chant whenever she went to see him play. A very brief nod was Dhanu's only acknowledgement of his family. But there was a new confidence in his step; his shoulders would widen, and there was a swag in his run.

His face grim with concentration, his straight hair standing up straighter on his head, eyes blazing with excitement, his thin chest heaving and drawing all his breath in, he swung the ball, kicking it with all his might. But unfortunately, it flew past the goal.

Slightly embarrassed, Dhanu did not wait but whizzed past his opponents, and he had the ball under his control again. But the opponents were smart. They outran him and took the ball from him, and soon, they were on the opposite side. He crashed against another player and went rolling down the field. But he was up and about in a second and rushing like the wind, he blew past everyone till he reached the ball. Before he could kick it, he crashed against another player and fell down yet again. This time, he did not get up immediately. He took his time; he took a shuddering breath in, filled his lungs with oxygen and then got up. He looked around and spied his family. He tried to walk normally, but he knew his game was over. With some difficulty, he walked towards them. Four disappointed faces looked towards him. He sat down beside them.

"Are you okay?" asked Shakuntala. "Is your leg hurting? Should I massage it?"

"No, no. I will be okay. Just resting it for a while. I will go back to the game," saying that he then gingerly touched his ankle. It seemed okay to his touch. The pain was there, but it was not excruciating. He decided to join the game.

Shouting his war cry, 'Jai Maha Kali Ayo Gorkhali,' he descended on the field like a hurricane. He wanted to score a goal for his team, which they very badly needed. And now there was no stopping him as he whizzed past one and all, his face streaked with mud with his shirt sticking to him. Sweat rolling down his face, he let out his war cry once again and kicked the ball. There was a deafening silence as the ball hit the side post and then went in. After that, Dhanu roared and then collapsed on the muddy field. His teammates heaped on him for what seemed like an eternity. They ran around the field in jubilation. After that, he ran towards his mother, who enveloped the grimy figure in a tight hug.

He couldn't believe they had won. His one last goal had done it. Looking at the rival team, he felt quite bad. They almost always lost. They would bear the brunt of all the jokes now till the next game.

Since he was grown up, he didn't have to ask his mother to buy them the sweets which stuck to their gums, to their teeth, to their hands and tasted like nothing in the world. He went ahead and bought them as it had become a ritual for the entire team, along with his siblings.

Dhan called his teammates, and they all celebrated with a handful of sticky, chewy sweets.

Amidst discussions as to what could have been done to get another goal, how unfair the referee had been and how next time they would do better, and so on and so forth, they had reached Mama's house.

The cousins ran out to greet Dhanu as the news of his winning goal reached home. Bikram had told all of them about that unbelievable goal, and there was a lot of excited noise. Everyone was happy, excited and ready to celebrate. To celebrate the great victory of Dhan Singh, they all had hot milk and tea. Mami fried pakoras, and the piping hot pakoras in the cold weather of Shimla tasted delicious. All of them quickly stuffed their mouths with the hot fritters, burning their tongues and relishing the crunchiness, not stopping till their aunt shooed the whole bunch out of the kitchen, telling them, “It’s over now. Everybody off to bed. This was dinner as well!” Amidst a lot of protests, the kitchen was closed. The children went straight to bed while Dhanu and Manu hurried back to the hostel.

After all that excitement, the hot milk and the pakoras, both of them snuggled into their quilts and were soon fast asleep. The warmth of the quilts, the cozy hostel room, and the warmth of the house on a cold blistering day put them into a deep contented slumber.

Chapter 8

MOTHER

There is a special place in heaven just for mothers like mine.

The next day was a warm sunny day, and it saw Draupadi make her way back to Solan. A lone and proud figure walking down the hill fearlessly, she was one feisty lady. Nothing deterred or scared her. She was happy during the weekend when her children came to Solan. For them, she would start cooking early in the morning, and by evening, she would have made all their favourite food.

Even through the week she was never lonely, as her relatives streamed in and out of the house. Solan was full of her relatives – her aunts, great aunts, and cousins. In fact, the whole village was related to her.

Her children would turn to her for advice. Whether they took it or not was a matter of choice. She adored her children but had no qualms about hitting them. It was not an easy task to bring up four boys without a father. She had often broken a prickly branch from a nearby tree and caned the living daylights out of the boys.

The boys with sore backsides, even in pain, found it hilarious that they were thrashed by the mother they adored and the mother who loved them. They would shake their heads and tell each other, "We will not repeat our mistakes. The caning is not worth it."

It made them do what she wanted, and they delivered. For a few days, they would work hard at what she wanted them to do – going regularly to school and working hard at the farm. But in a few days, all would be forgotten. Then, the whole scenario would be repeated again.

It was difficult to tame the children as they were a wild lot. They lived life on their own terms, but each one, as they became older, became responsible and settled down. In spite of the wildness, they had a streak of kindness in them, always ready to help people, listening to the sorrows of the older people, and dancing with joy with the younger children. The little village adored this family, the family that stood by the weak and the strong alike.

They helped sick people get medicines from Shimla and sometimes helped people till their land and harvest their crops.

This weekend, the children were coming to Solan. Draupadi was preparing their favourite food and she was waiting for them eagerly. The five of them loved their weekends in Solan. They would traipse up and down the hills, walking down towards their home from the bus stand.

The weekends were all about food, food and more food. The kids having slept on empty stomachs sometimes, loved their food. On Saturday and Sunday, they would gorge on food as though there was no tomorrow.

"What do you think Mother has made for lunch today?" asked Manu.

"Chana and puri. I know she knows I love chana and puri," said a salivating Dhanu.

"I think chicken curry and rice," said Bikram.

"And some aloo achaar," said Manu.

The children could go on and on talking about the food. When they came to meet Draupadi she really fed them well but at the same time made sure that they worked hard. After they would finish their lunch, they would go down to the fields to see how much work was done and how much needed to be done. They'd also work in the fields till evening and then would go back early morning to work again. It had become a routine for many years.

With the boys getting taller, stronger and older every day, it was getting easier for her to manage the work in the fields. They had turned into little men now. The fights among themselves had lessened but were getting fiercer.

As soon as the children reached home, they attacked the food ravenously. When the entire brood had been fed, she broke the news to them. A marriage proposal had come from a distant relative for Shakuntala. They had sent the boy's photo, which she showed the boys and Shakuntala. Very shyly, Shakuntala looked at the photo, and she liked what she saw. He was a good-looking young boy who was doing well in life.

Dhanu looked at his sister and asked her, "Do you like him?"

She answered, "He looks nice."

Before the other three boys could start teasing her, Dhanu gave them a look that told them to shut up.

"So should we say yes?"

"What does he do, mother?" asked Dhanu.

"He has a government job. I think you and Manu should go and meet the family. If you like them, then finalize the wedding. I think Shakuntala quite likes him," said his mother.

Draupadi had already shown the photo and spoken to her brother, Shamsher Singh, and they had had a long discussion about this match.

"I think we can leave on Sunday," decided Dhanu.

Bikram said, "I will also come. How come I get left out of all important decisions?"

So, it was decided that Bikram would go along as well.

Sunday morning saw the brothers smartly dressed in their nice clothes and shoes kept for special occasions. All that they lacked were nice hats; they would have looked like brown sahibs then.

They took a bus and, this time, sat inside, making sure their clothes didn't get crushed.

When they reached Shimla, they went to their uncle's house first. They rested for a while and then proceeded to the boy's house.

They were welcomed warmly. The family seemed warm and loving. The boy was extremely handsome. He had the looks of a romantic Indian film hero, and Dhanu and Bikram were quite impressed. M.B. Thapa was soft-spoken and worked in a government office. The brothers liked the boy and his family and decided that he was the boy for their sister and that she would be happy with him. And, of course, the huge amount of sweetmeats offered to them more than made up their minds about the boy. Sipping hot tea and eating all the snacks prepared for them, they sat discussing the wedding.

Dhanu was very happy that they had found the right boy for his sister. He had promised a palace for her which did not materialize, but at least he found a prince for her. He liked M.B. Thapa and was happy for his sister. He knew that his sister would be happy and would soon have her own little house and her own family.

"Let me discuss the dates for the wedding with the panditji in the village and get back to you," said Dhanu as they got up to leave.

Everyone was very happy that the marriage had been fixed. The family also wanted to come down to Solan to meet the family and meet the girl. It was decided they would come to Solan the following week. The panditji would be invited, too, and with the panditji there, the dates would be finalized.

This was a turning point in Dhanu's life. He had always shouldered the responsibilities of the family according to his age and capabilities, but now with adulthood came the serious decisions of life. All the small decisions made in childhood along with the mistakes had given him a wealth of experience. At this moment, he was very happy. He was happy for his sister as he knew she would like the boy as well.

Oh well, a wedding in the family! It was a sign from the heavens that happy times were here. The brothers took their leave and went back to their uncle's house.

Everyone wanted to know how the boy was and his family as well.

The whole family was very happy to know that the marriage was more or less fixed and that the boy's family would come down to Solan the following week.

Sure enough, they were in Solan in a week's time. Lunch was arranged by Draupadi and her sisters. Shyly, the boy and the girl met each other. Both the families were hugely amused by the filmy scene unfolding in front of their eyes. Shakuntala was looking at the boy from the corner of her eyes, and the boy knew he was being scrutinized by Draupadi, her mother and her two sisters.

The panditji decided to interrupt the romantic scene and said, “Next month is a good time for the wedding. We have a lot of auspicious dates.”

Thus, the date was decided. The panditji was fed well with food and hot milk, and Shakuntala was handed an envelope with Dakshina for the panditji, which she very shyly gave him. He blessed the couple and went his way.

Lunch was laid, and everyone ate with relish. There was a feeling of enjoyment. Wedding plans were already being discussed during lunch. Dhanu was not too sure how he would manage the finances, but at this point, he was just happy planning. They finished lunch, and the brothers walked down to the bus stop with their future brother-in-law and his family.

“I like Bajrog,” said M.B. Thapa.

Hiding a smile Dhanu thought, ‘I am sure you like Bajrog and especially now, when your dream girl lives here.’

Bikram replied, “Yes, it’s a nice village, away from the hustle-bustle of the town. It has its own charm. There is a lot of greenery.”

“Yes, a lot of greenery. The soil is very fertile here, and agriculture is one of the main occupations in this district. More than sixty per cent of people here are dependent on agriculture for their livelihoods. Earlier, we lived in Galhut village, but then we moved to Bajrog. The land here is also good. We still have land in Galhut, and we have a person who looks after the land and the house there. We call him Jhetoba as he is like family,” explained Dhanu.

Their bus was already waiting at the bus stand, and the brothers made sure that the boy and his family were seated before they started back home.

CHAPTER 9

SHAKUNTALA

Through every challenge and every victory, you have been there for me. My love for you is like a sweet scent always surrounding me with happiness.

The brothers had decided that it would be the best wedding ever organized in the village. It was their sister's marriage and the first wedding in their family.

The first thing the brothers did to finance the wedding was to sell their land in Gahlut. Their jhetoba also wanted to go back to Nepal, so this seemed the perfect solution. The whole house was decorated with flowers. *Halwais* were set up outside the house. The kitchen was on one side and a huge *shamiyana* was put up on the other side of the kitchen. The halwai had been preparing large laddoos, shakarparas, mathris and balushahi for one week now. Huge containers were being filled with the delicacies. These were being made for relatives who were coming from other states and for distributing to relatives who lived in the village.

The house was already full of aunts, uncles, their grandmother and cousins. Children of all ages ran amok, jumping up and down all over the place with their mothers running behind them, trying to control them. Cousins were busy trying out clothes while the elderly women of the family sat and cackled away with mugs of hot tea. Men, both old and young, sat on the charpoys with cups of tea and snacking on all the goodies.

On the other side of the house, the panditji sat and chanted, trying to complete a ritual. Bikram was given the duty of taking care of the panditji and his needs, so he ran around all the time – getting flowers, desi ghee, and turmeric for the puja, among other things. Manu and Kishan were looking after the relatives, seeing that they were seated and eating, serving endless cups of tea. They were in charge of the sleeping arrangements as well.

Draupadi was a little sad, though at the same time a little relieved. It was a time of mixed feelings. Every mother goes through this emotional ride when her daughter is getting married. You are sad and happy at the same time. Her daughter was getting married. For her, it was one of her wishes coming true – her daughter married and settled, secure in her own home, with a husband and soon little children.

Draupadi sighed a deep sigh, thanking God. She got up, picking up a little child sitting on the floor with dirty hands and a dirty face. She whacked him and, amidst his indignant crying, told his mother, “Go change his clothes. You young mothers don’t teach your children how to behave, and you don’t take care of them.” Saying that, she walked out, calling out for Dhanu. She wanted to know if everything was going according to plan and if everyone was dressed and ready for the baraat, which would be arriving any minute.

She herself looked like a regal figure wearing a beige-gold cotton saree. Her straight silver-grey hair was rolled into a bun and her face all soft and mushy for a change. She went and hugged her daughter, who promptly burst out crying.

Seeing her cry, all her brothers came and engulfed her in a huge hug. Six of them in a big group hug till they heard someone shout, "The baraat is here!" Then, everyone got into action. Sounds of merry-making could be heard in every corner of the house.

After the exchange of garlands, the bride and the bridegroom were taken to the *vedi* (an Indian altar where the *pheras* take place). Suddenly, they discovered that the panditji was nowhere to be seen. Dhanu was getting very stressed as the other brothers looked all over the place for him.

Then they spotted the panditji's wife sitting in one corner with a group of ladies and having hot tea. Dhanu walked up to her, "Where is Panditji?"

"He has gone home!"

"Why? He knows he has to conduct this wedding."

"He was not feeling too well. He had a slight fever, so he left."

Dhanu was furious, and he did not know how to react to her. He just turned to his brothers and said, "Go to his house and get him now! And I mean *now*."

In about half an hour, the shivering panditji bundled in to two blankets was back with the brothers. The mantras started, and the bride looked beautiful as she was tied in holy matrimony with M.B. Thapa.

But the most poignant part was the *bidai* (farewell of the bride). Seeing their mother cry, all the four brothers started crying. It was a sad scene and there was not a single person at that wedding who had a dry eye.

For the first time in her life, Draupadi felt very lonely. Shakuntala had always been there for her, when her workload became too much, when her emotions became too much... She would be there to hold her hand and support her as much as she could, but now suddenly, despite the fact that she had four boys, she felt bereft, as though a very integral part of her had been taken away. Dhanu could sense her tearful demeanour and clasped her tightly to him, promising to take care of her.

Chapter 10

ARMY

> The soldier is the Army. No army is better than its soldiers
>
> — George S. Patton Jr.

Before long, Dhan Singh Thapa joined the Indian Army. Born in Shimla on 10th April 1928, he was all of 21 years old when he joined the Army in the year 1949. His mother had always wanted her sons to serve the country, so he was fulfilling one of her wishes. He had an option to join the police force or the Army. He chose the Army.

When he was a child, his passion had been football, but as he grew older, he had given up all his aspirations of being a footballer. He had too many responsibilities to give his soul the freedom of a career of his own choice.

Having been a self-disciplined man throughout his life, the Army was a well-suited option for him. He enjoyed getting up early in the mornings, going for his exercises, walking for miles, and carrying heavy loads during his training period. He was easily able to undergo the rigorous training in the Army.

When he was posted in rough terrains or when he had to walk for miles, sometimes bearing the heat of the desert, at other times bearing the unbearable cold of the mountains, he could do it with ease. He had undergone so many hardships for most of his life that this seemed routine for him. But what the Army did to him was instil in him a great pride for his country. He realized then that he was made for the Army. To love and protect his country.

He was especially impressed by General Sam Manekshaw. On meeting Sam Manekshaw, also known as Sam Bahadur, his patriotic feelings grew by leaps and bounds. He admired General Manekshaw and always quoted him to his fellow officers and cadets. He admired the way General Manekshaw functioned with and against the political groups in power.

This particular quote from General Manekshaw: 'If a man said that he is not afraid of dying, he is either lying or is a Gorkha,' impressed Dhan Singh immensely. And the fact that it stated what a Gorkha was all about in one simple statement endeared him to the General. Dhan Singh Thapa was commissioned into the first battalion 8 Gorkhas in 1949 and received the temporary commission as a Second Lieutenant on 21st February 1951. He was promoted to a Lieutenant on 21st February 1953. He received the permanent commission as a Lieutenant on 29th September 1956, and was then promoted as a Captain on 21st February 1957.

The soldiers in his unit adored him. His word was law. He had that something about him which made his soldiers listen to him. They loved him and respected him. He just had to say it, and the job was done. He was an innovative man – nothing was too much or too little for him, and he constantly added innovation to the routine life in the Army. He was the kind of person who added excitement to life. If there were any events held in the unit, he would make sure that it would be special.

Soldiers are busy during wartime, actively involved in protecting their motherland and trying to stay alive. It was peacetime, which was a challenge. It was during this time that thoughts of killing and having killed disturbed many soldiers. These were the times the soldiers had to be kept busy, besides their ritualistic training, so that the thoughts of them dying, and of what their families would do and how they would survive could be kept at bay.

Dhan Singh made sure his men were busy, organizing rigorous training sessions, challenging games and events. He made sure every occasion was celebrated and that everyone would be involved.

He was known for the *Bada Khana* (official dinners in the Army) and dinners he would organize. He made sure the best food would be served in bada khanas, especially for the jawans. Though he enjoyed the sit-down dinners with his mates and his seniors just as much, he was the kind of person who would walk into the Army kitchen and tell the cooks what he wanted and how it was to be served exactly. It had to be presented in style, whether it was for the officers or for the jawans.

He would sit with the jawans, sing and dance with them. There was this particular gorkhali dance step in which he would twirl around gracefully to the music. This was a step for which he became famous in his unit.

One Dussehra, a special dinner was organized by the Commanding Officer. Thapa had made all the arrangements. He made the hall look like an Army warfare zone with Army nets thrown all around to add to the feeling. The snacks and drinks were served in huge wooden trays that needed four bearers. Dhan Singh was a people's person. He loved to talk and listen.

Having experienced life from close quarters, he could talk about anything under the sun.

The band started playing Dhan Singh's favourite song, and soon, he was on the dance floor with the CO's daughter. He asked her for this dance, and she graciously accepted. He, of course, did his favourite twirl, and she followed. Soon, all the youngsters of the regiment came onto the floor with their girlfriends and wives and friends. There was a lot of clapping, singing and dancing that went on late into the night.

***

The next day was the bada khana, and it was organized impeccably with the same detailing. He enjoyed himself immensely. He had an elephant's memory, and he would remember whose mother was unwell, who was saying whose brother would be joining the forces, and who needed extra money for his sister's wedding. He spoke to them about the problems and about the solutions. He spoke to them about everything. Even years later, he remembered and talked to them about it. The soldiers loved his concern, and thus, even before he became a hero, he was already a hero to them.

At the bada khana as well, it was he who started the momentum of dance and song. Soon, he had everyone doing his favourite Gorkha dance. This bada khana ended much in time because the next day was Monday. Monday morning started very early, and Dhan Singh was very particular about being punctual.

CHAPTER 11

IN LOVE

> It was love at first sight, at last sight, at ever and ever sight.
>
> — Vladimir Nabokov

Despite his busy schedule in the Army, Dhan Singh always managed to take out time for his family. He was always with them during his holidays, taking care of his mother, who was getting older, and encouraging his brothers to do more in life.

Lately, his mother had been pestering him to get married.

"No, Mother, let me get a permanent commission in the Army, and then we will see," Dhan Singh would reply dismissively.

One day, they were all sitting in their Solan house next to the fire, having eaten his favourite dal chawal and saag. They were all satiated and enjoying each other's company.Bikram urged his mother to show Dhan Singh a photo. He meanwhile was completely ignoring them and continuing to ply fire sticks to the already well-lit fire. His mother's sister Tara had sent them a photo – a group photo of four girls together. And they had put a cross on top of the girl's head. It was a black-and-white picture. The girl Shukla Thapa had long hair, and she made two plaits and put them upwards. She had a charming curl on her forehead and beautiful eyes lined with kajal. Those days, proposals were sent in such a manner. Sent through relatives, photos would be exchanged, and weddings planned.

Draupadi took the photo from the cupboard and gave it to Dhan Singh. "At least take a look," she said. "She looks like a very pretty girl. I believe she takes care of the whole house as her real mother left the family for a *sanstha,* so the father married again. The stepmother makes sure that she takes care of the house. She is only allowed to go to college after she finishes doing her housework. She also sings very well and plays the sitar." Having said that, she handed the picture over to Dhan Singh.

But before he could take the picture, Bikram grabbed the photo and told him if he wanted to see the picture, he would have to buy him new clothes.

Draupadi gave Bikram one whack, took the photo, and gave it to Dhan Singh, "If you behave like a child, you will get treated like one," she said.

Dhan Singh was looking at the group photo which had been sent by the girl's family. His heart suddenly started to do wild things in his chest. Shukla was really a beautiful girl; she looked like she could face all the happiness and problems life would hurl at them. His mother looked at him and asked, "You like her?"

"Which one is the girl?" he asked his mother very innocently.

"You guess," she said, chuckling away.

"Okay."

And he pointed to another girl. His mother burst out laughing. He loved the sound of her laughter as she had not seen much happiness. But she never let a joyous moment go. Smiling she told him, "No, it's the other girl. See they have put a cross, here take a look!"

She held the picture in such a way that he could not see the cross that marked the girl. But Dhan Singh knew who they were talking about. He just knew it. His heart knew it. Jumping up from the chair, he said, "Yes, yes and yes!"

The brothers looked at him in surprise. This was a new Dhan Singh they were seeing, but he couldn't be bothered. He was smiling from ear to ear. He was in love and in love with the photograph. What would happen if and when he finally met her! His mother was looking at him quizzically but got up and hugged him.

She said, "I will go and talk to the grandmother who sent this proposal and then let's see if they agree to this."

"Why won't they agree? My brother is a prince," boasted Bikram.

"Because they might want a king, silly," guffawed Manu.

"Quiet both of you! She will be your bhabhi, and you will have to respect her and do exactly what she tells you to do," said their mother.

"Why?" said the boisterous Manu.

"Because she will be like your mother," said the younger one.

"Only Draupadi is my mother. I acknowledge no other," said Manu.

"Oh, shut up, both of you! She will not live with the two of you. She will go with me wherever I am posted. You two can look after the farm and stay there!" retorted Dhan Singh.

"Look, Ma, he is not even married, and he is already siding with her. And she doesn't even know that he exists. What will happen when he gets married?" exclaimed Manu.

"And to top it all, I think she has a slight squint," said the over-imaginative Bikram.

"No problem, I love the squint. I think she looks beautiful."

"She looks a bit darkish," said the other brother.

" No problem. I love dusky skin."

"Her hair is too long."

"You guys are just jealous. Stop being jealous; let's welcome happiness and joy with our arms wide open. You will get married too. I will find beautiful brides for you when the time comes. And we will have the best wedding for you guys. All of Solan will be talking about them."

Having pacified his brothers, he turned to his mother and asked her, "How do we proceed?"

"Give me a nice photograph of yours, and I will send it to them. We'll wait for the reply," said his mother.

Dhan Singh quickly went to his suitcase, where a lot of his official files were kept.

He took out a picture in which he was in his breeches with his riding cap on, standing next to his favourite horse. He loved horse riding so he had kept a horse named Toofan (storm).

Dhan Singh looked pretty good in the photo. If truth be told, he looked better than a hero.

He handed the photo to his mother a little shyly. She looked at it and said, "My son is looking so handsome here."

"Thank you, mother." Dhan Singh nodded, running his fingers through his hair slightly self-consciously. Hugging his mother and brothers, he took their leave. He wanted to reach his unit much in time so that he could rest for a bit before the tough days ahead. Dhan Singh reached his bachelor's room, and saw that his orderly had prepared his bed. He had got his uniform ready for the next day. Lieutenant Dhan Singh was very particular about his uniform. He liked his uniform well-ironed, and his orderly knew that. He was very proud of his uniform and what it depicted. His orderly[1] asked him if he wanted any dinner.

The mess was just around the corner, and he would tell the cook to prepare Dhan Singh's favourite food for him. But Dhan Singh said he wasn't hungry.

"I will see you tomorrow morning," he told the orderly.

The orderly looked at Dhan Singh and thought that there was definitely something wrong. Dhan Singh never said 'no' to his food. He loved his food. There was definitely something amiss. 'Never mind, I will soon find out,' he thought.

He knew nothing was ever hidden from him. He would get to know in some time. Dhan Singh was an open book, and soon, the book would open up to him, and he would know.

Meanwhile, he said, "Good night, sir", and walked to his quarters.

The next day at the dinner table, Dhan Singh told his friend Lt Preet Kumar that he had fallen in love and most probably would get married to the girl in question. Few more of his friends had joined them for dinner there, and ensued a lot of commotion with everyone hugging him and congratulating him.

"But nothing is fixed yet," Dhan Singh kept protesting.

"*Aisa hi hota hai.* Next time you go on leave you most probably will come back with the bride," teased Preet Kumar.

His friends kept teasing him. They would make a cross with their fingers and then they would laugh embarrassing Dhan Singh. Finally, 'the iron man' as they fondly called him was in love. He was a man who just couldn't and wouldn't fall in love.

---

1 Now called buddy.

He had had no infatuations. He was a lady's man – one who loved to talk to them, dance with them entertain them, but not fall in love with them.

Having lived a tough life, he would not allow himself this luxury. He was totally focused on his career, but this time, his heart had not given him any choice. It had just taken charge of all his emotions.

His friends wanted to see the photograph and he promised them that at the next dinner, he would carry the photo with him.

He knew by the morning, the whole unit would learn about his love story. By now, the kitchen staff were abuzz with it. By the next day, the entire unit would know of it.

"Where does she live?"

"She lives in Joginder Nagar but is studying in Allahabad at present."

"When are you going to meet her?"

"Tomorrow!"

Smiling at his own joke, Dhan Singh told his friends, "If I had my way, I would go tomorrow and meet her."

"Oho, so Dhan Singh is in love. So what do you love the most about her?"

"Her smile, I think, no, maybe her hair. Actually, I have fallen in love with all of her. Okay, all of you, enough! When you guys go through this malady of love, I shall be beside you to help you recover, and I expect the same from you."

"Okay, last question, when are you planning to get married?"

"As soon as she says 'yes'," Dhan Singh guffawed loudly. He was known for his loud laughter. It could be heard half a mile away.

They all laughed with him, telling him that he better be careful. “She hasn’t even said ‘yes,’ and you are planning a wedding with her!”

After ragging him for a while longer, they left.

But the teasing went on. He would be talking to his Company Commander, and Preet Kumar would make the cross sign, and Lieutenant Dhan Singh would go red. He would be playing football in the evening, and he would come up behind him and show him a cross. All in all, they were giving him a tough time. But strangely, Dhan Singh was enjoying it.

Chapter 12

SHUKLA

> True beauty in a woman is reflected in her soul. It's the caring that she lovingly gives, the passion that she shows & the beauty of a woman only grows with passing years.
>
> — Audrey Hepburn

Meanwhile, Shukla, the girl in the crossed photograph, knew nothing of what was happening. She got up in the morning with a smile. She had this feeling that something good was going to happen that day. The feeling came to her when her real mother came to visit them. It happened to her when she got outstanding results. It happened to her again when her father took her shopping.

She was wondering what good was going to happen that day. But she'd better hurry as her stepmother would soon get up and start cribbing about her not having started making breakfast as yet.

She had lots of work, but before anything else, she had to take a bath and do her puja, a ritual her birth mother had instilled in her since she was a child. This she religiously followed. Humming her favourite bhajan, she completed her prayers and was serving breakfast to her father when her grandmother bustled in.

Her grandmother was huge but she was beautiful. She had a gorgeous unlined face that never aged. Shukla remembered her like this when she was a child, and as she grew older the face of her granny remained the same.

She told her father, "A proposal has come for Shukla!" Shukla almost dropped the plate of parathas that she was serving her father.

She hid behind the kitchen door, dying to learn the details. She wanted to know more about the boy. Where was he from? What did he do? How educated was he? Was he rich? Was he fair? Was he tall? All these questions whirled around her head. But she dared not come out and ask her father all these questions.

It was not expected of her. Her father would throw a royal fit, and she would never hear the end of it. "The photo looks nice, and if he is an officer in the Army, that would also be good. We know the family; that is another plus point. It seems like a good proposal," pondered her father.

Shukla almost fainted with excitement. She was dying to see the photograph. She frantically signalled to her cousin to come out, and when she did, she pounced on her. "Where is the photo?"
"It's with uncle."

"What does he look like?"

"He's a little darkish and has a slight squint."

Shukla was ready to burst into tears. I can't marry a squint-eyed ugly man, she thought to herself. Wait till I catch hold of my grandmother. I will make sure that she makes sure that this match goes no further.

As soon as her father left for the office, she went all teary-eyed to her grandmother, "How could you do this to me?" she wailed. "Not you. I never expected you to do this to me. How can you get a proposal of this ugly, squint-eyed man for me? I will never marry him, never!"

"What are you talking about?" said her curious grandmother, wondering why Shukla was crying.

Shukla was a girl of substance. She did not cry easily. A very strong girl, she knew what she wanted in life. Her real mother had joined a religious sect and left home when Shukla and her brother Shankar had been very young. Her father had married again. Her stepmother was not the typical evil stepmother, but neither was she close to a real mother. Shukla had grown up emotionally and physically all by herself. She had to deal with happy and sad emotions on her own. So, she was not the type of girl to start crying for no reason. Her grandmother called her and hugged her.

"No, don't hug me. You people don't really love me. If my mother would have been here, she would not have allowed this. You people just want to get rid of me and be done with your responsibility."

"Can you tell me why are you upset?" asked her grandmother.

She went to her grandmother, hugged her, and started crying. "I cannot marry him if he is squint-eyed. How could you even select a man like that for me?" She went on crying with huge tears rolling down her cheeks.

"He is not like that at all. He is a good man and a good-looking man. You will be a lucky woman if he decides that he likes you and wants to marry you."

"I will run away. I am not scared of anyone. I will not marry just anybody... how can you make such a decision without my permission? I, at least, need to see him. Show me that photo!" she raved and ranted.

"Don't worry, my little princess. Once your father comes back, you can see the photo, and you can decide whether you like him or not. Don't get upset. Go to college, and trust me," said her grandmother.

Chapter 13

TEMPER

Girls who have a short temper mostly have innocent hearts.

Shukla was angry. Very angry, but she was very upset as well. She didn't realize that the reason for her anger was right behind her.

Lieutenant Dhan Singh had decided to come to Allahabad to see his dream girl in person. He had reached Allahabad the previous night, and in the morning, he had come to her college – Prayag Mahavidyalaya Vidyapeeth. He was waiting outside the college to catch a glimpse of her.

Suddenly, he saw her in a pink salwar kameez with her dupatta flying in the air as the rickshaw driver swerved to avoid a cyclist. He was not disappointed. She was more beautiful than her photograph. With a flawless complexion, and beautiful long hair with loose strands making their way out of her plait, flying all over her face. He could make out she was in a temper. Angrily she was handing the money to the rickshaw puller who couldn't stop staring at her; he was saying something to her. Dhan Singh stepped forward to listen to what he was saying.

The rickshaw puller said, *"Aap se kuch kahe?"* (Can I say something to you?)

"Aap bolo (you say)," she replied.

"Aap bura to nahi manoge?" (I hope you won't mind?)

Shukla said, annoyed, *"Bolo!"*

"*Aap bahut khubsurat hai,*" (You are very beautiful) he blurted out.

Dhan Singh thought the poor rickshaw puller was not going to be spared. But it was a lucky day for him because Shukla was not in the mood to have any kind of showdown with anybody. She just jumped off the rickshaw and strode off. The shy, angry girl stamping around college had stomped on his heart and had left her footmarks in it.

He waited outside her college and had breakfast at one of the roadside stalls close to the college. He hadn't realized how hungry he was. He relished his egg and bun with the tea. Everything tasted so good, maybe because he was feeling so upbeat. There was a rainbow in his heart which was colouring him red – the colour of love.

Dhan Singh struck up a conversation with Raju, the man who was looking after the food stall as he waited. He was most interesting. His knowledge was immense, and soon, he regaled Thapa with the Allahabad political scenario.

Just before lunchtime, Shukla rushed out of the college. 'Oh my! Madam is still in a temper,' he thought. He saw her emerging from the college gates and took in the sight of her. He wanted to memorize each and every feature. He walked behind Shukla and her friends. She was gesticulating angrily, and he could overhear a few sentences. He chuckled at the thought that soon he would be the one listening to her tales of woe.

Well, soon enough.

He was so lost in his thoughts that before he knew it, he was almost upon the group of girls. One of the girls, a bossy girl, caught hold of his hand and said, “I saw you following us. What do you want?”

Dhan Singh, always quick on the uptake, said, “*Army officer ke sath is tarah ka bartaav? Hum duty pe hain, madam.*” (How are you behaving with an Army officer? I am on duty, madam.)

Taken aback, the girl said, “*Sir, aapke liye salute to banta hai.*”

And giggling, all of them saluted him. Meanwhile Shukla had hailed a rickshaw and had left. She wanted to reach home and see that photograph. The thought of that picture was haunting her.

Lunchtime was over. Everyone had finished lunch, but there was no sign of her father. Waiting impatiently for her father, she couldn’t concentrate on anything. She tried to study but couldn’t. She put on the radio, but it irritated her, so she switched it off.

Finally, she slept off. Waking up, she heard her father telling his wife to give him dinner. She looked out of the window. It was pitch dark, and the sky had turned a deep purple. Rushing down, she waited in the hallway. She knew that he had heard her and would soon call for her. Sure enough, he called her, “Shukla, come here!”

She came slowly, her eyes begging him to tell her otherwise. But he seemed delighted and very happily informed her.

“I have fixed your wedding. It will be held next month on the 5th of May.”

Shukla gulped her fear down. If she didn’t speak, then it would be too late so she gathered all her ounces of strength and said with great determination, “But I have not met the boy nor have I seen the boy’s photograph.”

"Don't you trust me?" he said, swallowing a bite of rice and dal.

This was getting difficult. She knew this was the moment to make it or break it.

Shukla respected her father and knew that eventually she would do what he asked her to do. But she was a determined woman. There was no harm in trying.

"Pitaji, I have to marry the boy. I have to spend my entire life with him, how can I let you take this decision for me? I don't even know what he looks like. I haven't even met him once. At least let me meet him once," beseeched Shukla.

"Nothing like this happens in our *khandaan*. Marriages are planned by the elders of the family," said her father sternly.

"Am I asking for too much if I say I want to see his photo or if I could meet him once?"

"What difference will it make? When I say that the marriage is fixed, it is fixed. You might see the photo and decide that you don't like the boy, then what? I have given my word now, I can't break that."

Sitting down to have dinner with her stepmother and grandmother, she couldn't swallow the food. She took a sip of water and forced the dal and rice to go down her throat. All the while, she wanted to throw that plate on the wall. She wanted to scream and shout and take out all her anger. But she managed to finish the handful of rice and dal which her stepmother had put out for her.

Excusing herself, she went to her room and lay down. In the haven of her room, the tears came gushing out. There was no one to comfort her, and she cried till she exhausted herself and fell into a deep slumber.

In the morning, the warm golden light of the sun filled her room. She wished it could fill her heart and drive away the depressing blues. She had a terrible feeling of emptiness within her.

While praying to God that morning, she told him, "I have no choice, but yes, I know you will take care of me. You have done that all through my life, and you will do so always."

She felt much better when she went down for breakfast. She got a surprise. Her father forbade her from going to college any longer. In any case, she had finished her eleventh, which was called Inter in those days, and these were her last days in college.

The marriage had been fixed, and she would now get busy getting her trousseau ready. That afternoon, there was another surprise for her. Her father had sent the photograph of the boy through her grandmother. He looked very handsome; it didn't seem like he had a squint. In the photo, he was wearing a riding hat and breeches and stood holding a horse. A wave of happiness flowed through her. She sat down on the bed, staring at the picture.

She went to her cousin and said, "He doesn't have a squint."

"No, but I thought in the photo he looked slightly squintish!" she said as she walked out. The squint had really upset Shukla, and now she wanted to slap her cousin. But in retrospect, she was so happy she didn't really care. She fell in love with the photo. She finally had her own Prince Charming. Those days to fall in love with photographs was the done thing!

Inspired by Hindi movies, she even did a waltz with the photo; the only thing lacking in this scene was the music and the heroine singing.

Chapter 14

PREPARATIONS

> The best love is the kind that awakens the soul and makes us reach for more, that plants a fire in our hearts and brings peace to our minds.
>
> — Nicholas Sparks

A month had flown by. Time has a habit of moving fast, especially when you want it to go slow. Shukla wanted to do so much, but her plans were going awry with her having so little time. Shukla and her dad shopped for her trousseau together. All her sarees and her jewellery had been bought by her father. For her wedding day, her father had bought her a gorgeous beige saree. Those days, brides only wore red, but her father had a mind of his own and bought her a lovely gold beige saree. He had impeccable taste. The shopkeeper insisted she buy a red saree, but he wanted something different for his daughter.

After going through almost a hundred sarees, he chose a beige Banarasi saree with a beautiful gold border. Shukla loved the saree. They bought a few other sarees as well. Her father, Har Bahadur, insisted, "You will be attending a lot of Army functions and dinners. You must be appropriately dressed."

Together, they went to another shop and picked up a few more sarees.

Shukla loved her sarees, but she was tired. Tired and anxious about the coming of the most important date of her life. But she was unbearably joyous at the same time.

"Pitaji, can we go home now? I am tired."

Shukla knew she would have to back home and organize dinner so she did not want to over tire herself.

She was still helping around the house, even though her brother Shankar had said that no more work for her because she was getting married, so she should enjoy her last few days at her parent's house. But she insisted on being in the kitchen, helping her stepmother. Her father ushered a rickshaw, and in less than ten minutes, they were home. She rested for a while and then went to the kitchen to get dinner ready. After dinner, her father sat down with a paper and pen to make a to-do list for the preparations.

The next day, she got up to the sun shining brilliantly. It was as though nature wanted to share her happiness. Everything around her glowed and shone. She herself would smile and laugh for no rhyme or reason and then would tell herself, "What's wrong with you, Shukla? Stop it!"

Hurriedly, she went to the kitchen to make breakfast for everyone. Giggling to herself, Shukla went to the kitchen, hugged her stepmother and said, "Don't worry, I am here. I have had my bath, and my puja is done. Now I am all yours."

Her stepmother looked at her, amused, "Well, love has definitely changed you. Okay, your father is about to come. He wants eggs and some tea for breakfast."

Shukla quickly made the eggs and fried some parathas for him. Soon, the tea was ready. She went out to the dining room with his breakfast tray. He called her to him, hugged her and said, "Who is going to look after me when you go away?"

She looked at him in surprise. He had always seemed so strong a figure. Someone she was frightened of. Someone who had told her what was right and wrong, not someone who she could confide in. There was always a respectful distance between them. But today, he seemed like any other father whose daughter was going to get married and leave. He somehow seemed frail and teary-eyed.

She hugged him and said, "I'm always there for you, Baba. You just have to shout, and I will be here."

Suddenly, she seemed to be the stronger one. How roles reverse in life. Subtly, but change they do. Blessing her, her father Har Bahadur Thapa sat down for breakfast.

Now, it was Shankar's turn. "I will go with you. I cannot live without you," he said as his emotions got the better of him.

Shukla and her brother were very close. He had always taken care of her, and she in turn of him. Her father told him to keep quiet, but Shukla signalled to him, "Yes, I will take you with me." Shukla and her family had shifted to Joginder Nagar. The wedding was to take place there. Joginder Nagar was a municipality in the Mandi district of Himachal Pradesh and was named after Raja Joginder. It was a small beautiful sleepy town. It had beautiful streams and it was surrounded by hills and mountains. The mountains were covered with dense pine forests. It was very scenic and romantic, a filmmaker's dream location. And since it was not 'discovered' as yet, it was still pristine.

At home, there was a buzz of activities. The halwais were being tested, and their food was being tasted. The decorators were in and out of the house. A lot of plans were being shown to Shukla and her father, Har Bahadur Singh Thapa. Arrangements were being made to put up the guests. Then there were arrangements to be made for the bridegroom's side of the family. They would be coming to Joginder Nagar on the 1st of May 1955, four days before the wedding.

There was excitement in the air. Her father was organizing everything. He had found a huge house for the bridegroom and his family, and they had been renting it for ten days. The house was semi-furnished, and the rest of the arrangements were being made.

The house was quite big, and it had a huge garden in the front. Many functions could take place there. The rooms were huge and airy, with lots of sunshine coming through the French windows. They were going to be there for ten days. There were functions almost every day. The huge house seemed just right for the wedding.

It was the first of May and Lieutenant Dhan Singh Thapa was arriving in Joginder Nagar in the evening. The house was gleaming and shining like a new bride in all her glory. It had been decorated with flowers and multitude of lights. All kinds of food were being made for the baratis. The smell of food permeating from the house was making everyone's mouth water.

Shukla's little cousins would come in screaming and shouting, *"Baraat aai gayo!"* meaning 'they are here' and this they shouted when any bus came within sight. The bus would go off, and then there would be silence till these little children saw the next bus. Then, they would start all over again. Finally, when their bus did arrive, the children went ballistic. Shukla's father and brother, along with a few uncles, went to greet them.

The evening tea had been arranged at the house. The panditji who had come with the bridegroom had been quite sick on the way. He had been given some medicines and told to go and rest in his room.

The whole house was all lit up, and it looked straight out of a fairy tale. Bikram and Manu checked the rooms and allocated them to all the cousins and uncles. The younger cousins had decided to put mattresses or beds on the floor in the sitting room and sleep there. The elders were given rooms on the ground floor, and the ones on the first floor were given to couples and their children.

Har Bahadur Thapa sat with Dhan Singh's mother in the sitting room, sipping tea and discussing the plans for the wedding.

The next day, there was Ganesh puja. Kasaar laddoos were specially made on the day. They were round balls of rice and sugar, made specially during weddings.

So the next day, a small havan and Ganesh puja were held in both houses. Shukla got up early in the morning and dressed in a pink saree. Her gleaming hair was tied in one single plait. Flowers were plaited into her hair. She wore only a pair of ruby earrings, which she had gotten from her mother. Her mother had belonged to the Rana royal family from Nepal. They had come to India with all their jewellery and a lot of gold. There were stories that her mother's family had come with a whole entourage of families. And these families had come laden with jewels packed in sacks carried by mules.

So when her mother got married, she was given some of the jewellery. She had passed down some of it to her daughter. Shukla looked beautiful in her simplicity.

With pink glass bangles on her wrists, a simple pink saree and some kajal lining her eyes, smelling of roses with one pink bindi and pink lipstick, she was ready. Her father and brother were already there with the panditji. Shankar was overseeing the sitting arrangements for the guests.

Mattresses were being put out, and clean sheets were being spread on them. Her father signalled to her to sit beside him. She walked slowly and shyly towards him. This was the beginning of the most important chapter in her life, and she wanted to start it with Ganesh's prayers. She sat down next to her father, and her stepmother sat down next to her. The panditji started the prayers, and soon, her cousins, aunts, uncles, and grandparents joined in. The prayers were followed by lunch served under a huge shamiyana in the garden.

By the evening, everyone was totally exhausted. 'Today is just the first day and I'm so tired,' thought Shukla. 'What is going to be my condition after seven days of celebrations?'

Her father called her. With one look at her exhausted face, he said, "You go to your room and rest. Shankar will get you your dinner."

Shukla, before anyone else could catch hold of her, quickly went to her room. She rested for a while and before long she was fast sleep. She only got up when Shankar came knocking with a plateful of food. She was surprised to find that she was very hungry. She finished everything on her plate and promptly went back to sleep.

In the other house, the prayers and havan were completed. There was a lot of music and dancing. The brothers and cousins sat together, singing songs. Others started dancing. Snacks were being sent out in generous amounts. It was quite late when everyone went to sleep exhausted. They were, however, rudely awakened by Draupadi shouting at them, "Who told you to stay up so late? The panditji is going to be here soon, and none of you have had a bath. Arrangements for the panditji haven't been made either!"

She was getting really furious. She did not want to make any kind of compromises with the religious rituals. Luckily for the whole lot, Dhan Singh came down, all bathed and ready to handle the situation.

"Can I have a cup of tea first before I sit down with the panditji?" he asked.

"No. You finish the puja, and only then can you drink and eat anything."

Dhan Singh walked out irritated. He loved his hot cup of tea, but knowing his mother, he knew she meant business. He got up and went outside to greet the panditji. His sister was also already present handing him water, tikka, oil, *deubo* (a holy grass) along with the other things he needed. Dhan Singh sat down and the panditji started the rituals. After the puja they were going to Shukla's house and the engagement was going to take place.

It was the 3rd of May. It was the day of their engagement. There was a flurry of activities at the bride's house. Shankar was in a tizzy. It seemed to him everyone wanted him for something or the other. He wanted to go and get dressed but was just not able to get away.

"Shankar, where is my thaali?" the panditji shouted.

"Shankar, can you check how much time will the baraatis take to reach?" his father was saying.

"Shankar bhaiya, should I serve the halwa with the food or serve it later?" the halwai was calling out to him.

Shankar just left everyone and escaped to his room. He lay

Lt Col Dhan Singh Thapa,
PVC was commissioned into
1/8 Gorkha Rifles in 1949.

Shukla Thapa,
wife of Lt Col Dhan Singh Thapa,
PVC.

From his first posting in Mathura.

The photograph first sent to
Mrs Shukla Thapa.

At the Indian Military Academy, Dehradun.

Addressing his men, gearing up for the Sino-Indian War of 1962.

Relaxing with other soldiers *(second from right)*.

With his idol,
Field Marshal **Sam Manekshaw.**

Dr Sarvepalli Radhakrishnan,
the then Honourable President of India, awarded the Param Vir Chakra – India's highest military decoration – to Major Dhan Singh Thapa.

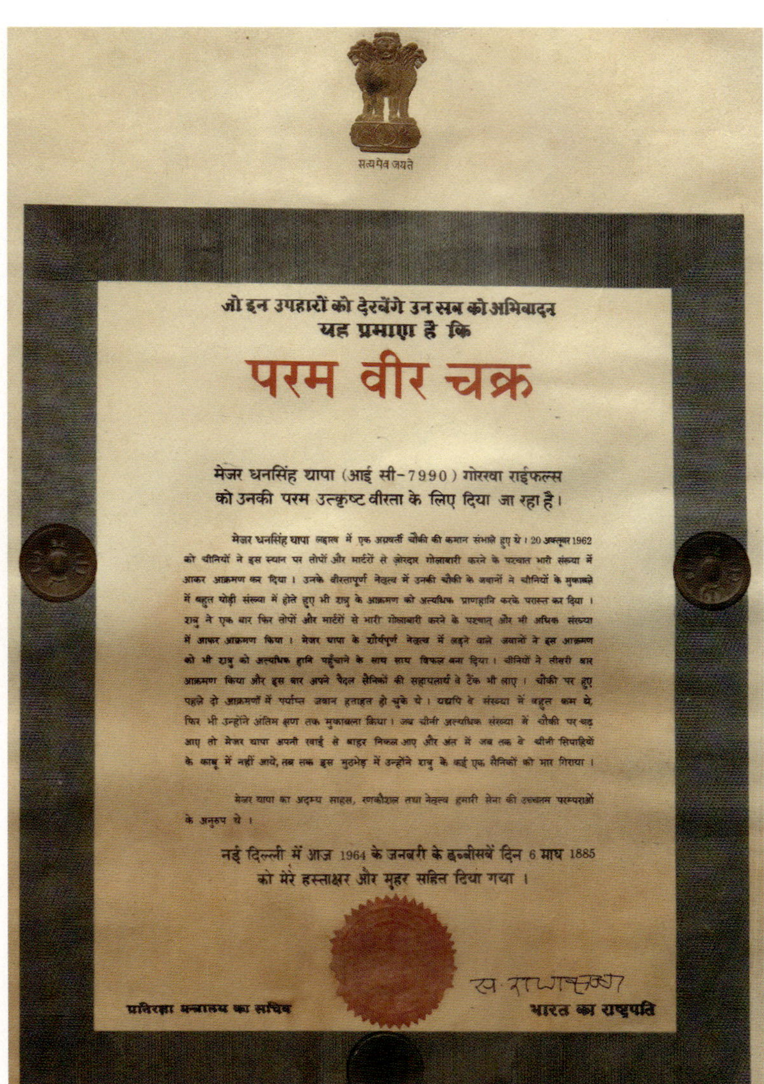

सत्यमेव जयते

जो इन उपहारों को देखेंगे उन सब को अभिवादन
यह प्रमाण है कि

परम वीर चक्र

मेजर धनसिंह थापा (आई सी-7990) गोरखा राईफल्स
को उनकी परम उत्कृष्ट वीरता के लिए दिया जा रहा है।

मेजर धनसिंह थापा लद्दाख में एक अग्रवर्ती चौकी की कमान संभाले हुए थे। 20 अक्तूबर 1962 को चीनियों ने इस स्थान पर तोपों और मार्टरों से ज़ोरदार गोलाबारी करने के पश्चात भारी संख्या में आकर आक्रमण कर दिया। उनके वीरतापूर्ण नेतृत्व में उनकी चौकी के जवानों ने चीनियों के मुकाबले में बहुत थोड़ी संख्या में होते हुए भी शत्रु के आक्रमण को अत्यधिक प्राणहानि करके परास्त कर दिया। शत्रु ने एक बार फिर तोपों और मार्टरों से भारी गोलाबारी करने के पश्चात् और भी अधिक संख्या में आकर आक्रमण किया। मेजर थापा के शौर्यपूर्ण नेतृत्व में लड़ने वाले जवानों ने इस आक्रमण को भी शत्रु को अत्यधिक हानि पहुँचाने के साथ साथ विफल बना दिया। चीनियों ने तीसरी बार आक्रमण किया और इस बार अपने पैदल सैनिकों की सहायतार्थ वे टैंक भी लाए। चौकी पर हुए पहले दो आक्रमणों में पर्याप्त जवान हताहत हो चुके थे। यद्यपि वे संख्या में बहुत कम थे, फिर भी उन्होंने अंतिम क्षण तक मुकाबला किया। जब चीनी अत्यधिक संख्या में चौकी पर चढ़ आए तो मेजर थापा अपनी खाई से बाहर निकल आए और अंत में जब तक वे चीनी सिपाहियों के काबू में नहीं आये, तब तक इस मुठभेड़ में उन्होंने शत्रु के कई एक सैनिकों को मार गिराया।

मेजर थापा का अदम्य साहस, रणकौशल तथा नेतृत्व हमारी सेना की उच्चतम परम्पराओं के अनुरूप थे।

नई दिल्ली में आज 1964 के जनवरी के छब्बीसवें दिन 6 माघ 1885
को मेरे हस्ताक्षर और मुहर सहित दिया गया।

प्रतिरक्षा मन्त्रालय का सचिव

भारत का राष्ट्रपति

The Citation of the **Param Vir Chakra** awarded
to Maj Dhan Singh Thapa.

Maj Dhan Singh Thapa during the
Republic Day celebrations

Maj Dhan Singh Thapa, PVC
(centre, in white) as an instructor at IMA in 1964.

Red Cross receives third list of Indian POWs

The list of POWs *(Prisoners of War)* where Maj Thapa's name was revealed.

Bust of Lt Col Dhan Singh Thapa,
PVC at Param Yodha Sthal in Delhi.

down on his bed for ten minutes taking deep breaths and then surfaced. He took a quick shower and dived back into the chaos. Dhan Singh and family had arrived and were sitting in the living room with Har Bahadur Thapa and his family. They were waiting for Shukla.

Shukla had decided to wear a simple red saree with a thin gold border for the engagement. She wore simple gold jewellery with a small tikka on her forehead. Entering the room with Shankar, she folded her hands without looking at anyone. Her heart was beating so loudly that she was sure everyone around her could hear it.

Dhan Singh's heart did a violent somersault, but he handled it well. His expression was worth looking at. He sat there with his mouth open and kept looking at her. It was Manu who told him, "Daaji, it's okay to close your mouth now. In two days' time, she will be with you forever."

At this comment, both the brothers burst out laughing. Dhan Singh's booming laughter could be heard by half of Joginder Nagar.

The grandmother had just regaled the tale of how Shukla's cousin had misled Shukla about how he looked and how upset she had been. This angered Dhan Singh. He could at times just blow up so it was lucky that the cousin had decided to give the wedding a miss. Otherwise, there was no way Dhan Singh would have spared her. Another absentee in the wedding was Shukla's birth mother.

Shukla was quite upset about it, but everything had happened too fast. Her mother wrote to Shukla and said that it was too short a notice for her to come, but her blessings would always be with her. Shukla had not spent too much time with her, so she was quite okay with it. All her growing years, she had not been there for her, and she had learnt to deal with life on her own.

The ceremony had started with all of the family members putting tikka with rice and vermillion on the couple's foreheads. So before they actually exchanged the gold ring, they had to exchange a grass ring known as *kusha* ring. In Hinduism, kusha grass is holy and in Gorkhali culture, the kusha ring is exchanged before the gold ring. The panditji performed all the traditional rituals with great aplomb, finally blessing the couple after they were completed.

Shukla had sat through the ceremony with her eyes down and had not spoken a word to anyone. The panditji blessed the couple with a long happy life. He made them exchange their rings, which were two simple gold bands. The relatives walked down to them and made the couple eat sweetmeats and gave them gifts.

Food had been served to the panditji by Shankar. But he was a little grumpy and not very happy with the *dakshina* given to him. Dhan Singh felt bad that the panditji was not happy. He nudged his mother and whispered to her to go and give panditji some more dakshina.

She quickly got up and went to the panditji and said with folded hands, "Please bless the couple, panditji, with a happy and joyous future."

She handed him an envelope, which pacified him, and he happily blessed the couple once again. After having his food and a glass of hot milk, he left. Shukla only spoke when the food was being laid. She was very hungry, so she told Shankar, who had been by her side throughout, to go get some food for her. The minute he got up to go, Dhan Singh said softly, "You are looking very beautiful!"

She gulped and nervously looked around, but there was no one, so she said, "Thank you."

"The red colour really suits you. After marriage, I will mostly buy red clothes for you." Shukla blushed and said, "Is red your favourite colour?"

Dhan Singh, looking quizzically at her, replied, "From now on." Saying that, Dhan Singh took her hand in his hand and asked, "Do you like the ring?"

Getting bolder by the minute, she said, "I love it, and you?"

"I will never remove this ring," he replied, putting his hand next to his heart. That made her blush, but she mustered the courage to say, "Neither will I."

Dhan Singh was delirious with happiness. She was more than he had dreamt about. The way she handled herself was exactly the way he had imagined she would do so. Simply and yet so gracefully.

Meanwhile, Shankar came back with a plate full of aloo, puri, chana, raita, pulao and pumpkin. She looked at the heaped plate and got furious.

She looked at him and said, "Can I eat so much?"

"I will eat a bit, and you can eat the remaining," said Shankar.

"No, get me a fresh plate and get me a small portion. I cannot eat so much."

Dhan Singh was most amused. Everything about her amused him. He looked pitifully at Shankar going back and forth and thought to himself that in a few days, he would be doing that for her. He was happy at the prospect. Love is like that. It makes you want to do things for your loved ones.

Dhan Singh asked her, "So you like aloo puri? I saw that on your plate."

"Yes, that is my all-time favourite. What is your favourite food?"

"I love every kind of food. I am a foodie. I am very fond of sweets and can eat any amount of them. Sweets are my weakness!"

Shukla smiled at the passion in his voice.

Shankar came back with a plate with only aloo puri in it. Shukla gave him an angry stare and he laughed and said, "Now what?"

Dhan Singh looked at her plate and guffawed loudly. His reverberating infectious laughter made everyone look at him.

Dhan Singh, indicating his full plate, said, "You can eat from my plate."

"No, thank you," she replied.

Finishing her lone puri, she told Shankar to get more, "And get the gobi aloo sabji and a gulab jamun, too."

Shankar lumbered off grumpily, but he never refused his sister anything. He adored her and had protected her umpteen times from their stepmom, who would not dare say anything to him. He was the darling boy of the family, and no one said anything to him. He, in turn, would do anything for his sister, though he was not there all the time to take care of her. But when he was, he treated her like a princess.

The rice and the vermillion tikka on her forehead started falling on her nose.

Dhan Singh took out his white handkerchief and wiped her nose. Shukla was mortified, wondering if anyone was looking at them. Very self-consciously, she looked around.

She very shyly said, “Don’t do that; everybody is looking.” Her blushes were endearing.

He looked at her, “We are engaged and I am only wiping this tikka from your nose.” Before she could reply Shankar was back with her plate.

So that he could talk more with her, he asked Shankar to get him a gulab jamun. Shankar caught sight of Bikram and delegated the job to him as he wanted to finish his dinner in peace.

Shukla nudged Shankar, “You go. He has asked you to get it.”

A very disgruntled Shankar got up and left his half-eaten food on the plate. Dhan Singh was very impressed to see that Shukla was a woman of control. When you are in love, everything about the person you love is wonderful. Nothing can be wrong about that person.

Seeing her sitting with clasped hands, he unwound her hands very gently and said, “Relax, it is your ring ceremony. Enjoy it! I promise you that you will never have a reason to get stressed again.”

‘He is right. We are getting married. I have no reason to stress myself unnecessarily,’ she calmed herself. She finished her meal and made Shankar get up and go get a cold drink for her. Soon, the festivities were over. It was time for Dhan Singh and his family to go back to their own lodgings. The next day was the mehendi ceremony and it would certainly be another long day.

Chapter 15

MEHENDI

> All love is capable of energising wishes into reality, but love between two people whose personal auras are harmoniously blended creates the kind of vibration poets write about and can manifest magic.

The day of mehendi dawned nice and bright. The sun was shining in all its glory. The white clouds dotting the sky were doing a sacred dance changing their shapes constantly, as though in slow motion. It was as though the couple was being blessed by the gods as well as the universe.

The mehendi day is a day of fun. It is celebrated with songs, music, and good food. The bride and her friends are gifted bangles and bindis. On this day, the sister-in-law in the family applies mehendi on the bride's hands and feet. Also, there are girls who put mehendi for a fee. In those days, relatives applied mehendi to each other. There is a superstition about mehendi; they say if your mehendi is dark, then your husband and mother-in-law will really love you. So, most brides keep the mehendi for a long time, and the longer you keep it, the darker it gets.

Shukla sat with flowers braided in her hair, as mehendi was applied to her hands and feet. Instead of jewellery, she was wearing flowers around her neck and in her ears.

She was wearing a yellow saree and had put a yellow bindi on her forehead. She looked stunning. Yellow was a colour that really suited her. The simplicity of the attire added to her beauty and how.

Her friends were also getting mehndi applied on their hands. And the ones who hadn't were feeding the ones who had, as they couldn't afford to spoil the wet paste on their hands and feet.

On this day, a mandap, where the bride and the groom sit and get married, is also made. The mandap is made of banana tree branches, which are dug into the ground in four corners, making the four pillars of the mandap. This mandap is then decorated with pots filled with water and garlands of mango leaves, coconut and banana leaves. In the centre is the *havan kund*, where the wedding havan puja is done.

As the mandap was being made for the wedding ceremony, Shukla and her friends were getting their mehendi done. Some friends were singing while others were dancing in merriment. The men meanwhile were busy sampling all the sweets that had been made for the wedding weeks ago.

Shukla's mehendi had dried and she scraped it to see how dark it was. Seeing that colour was quite dark she scraped it all off and oiled her hands.

Since she had hardly eaten any lunch as it was difficult to eat with someone else feeding her, she picked up a plate and served herself a huge helping of dal, chawal, sabzi, paratha and started to eat.

Her friends teased her, "Don't eat so much. You will become fat."

She laughed and said, "I will never put on weight. I have too much energy. I will sweat it out."

With flowers in her hair and hands she looked like a beautiful painting. She smilingly looked at the heaped food in her plate. There were no compromises where food was concerned.

"What's for dessert?"

"Your favourite kheer," said Shankar, who had just walked up to sit with them.

"His favourite, too," said Shukla shyly.

"Oh, so you know that as well," teased Shankar.

"He mentioned it to me once," said Shukla airily. She clammed up, seeing her father walking towards them.

He told Shukla, "Don't tire yourself too much. Tomorrow is the big day. The puja starts in the morning and will go on till the afternoon. And then in the evening is the wedding ceremony."

Shukla blushed, "Yes, Pitaji. I was just going to rest in my room."

Amidst a lot of giggling, Shukla and her friends went to her room.

The 5th of May 1955 was the happiest of days for Shukla.

According to William Lyon Phelps too, 'The highest happiness on Earth is the happiness of marriage.'

Dhan Singh's day started with a puja as well. A paste of freshly pounded turmeric was applied to the bride and the groom in their respective houses. It started in the groom's house where this turmeric paste is rubbed on to the groom and then a small amount of that is removed from his body and sent to the bride's house to be applied to the bride by her relatives. The paste is called *bukwa*.

Shukla's cousins had come to collect the bukwa, all of them giggling away looking at Dhan Singh enjoying the haldi ceremony. All his brothers were trying to remove his shirt and trying to apply the bukwa on his face and on his clothes.

Draupadi told them, “Have some tea.”

“No, we are in a rush. We have to start the same ceremony there as well.” Saying that, the girls hurried off.

Shukla had worn a peach-coloured saree. One corner of the shamiana had been decorated with yellow flowers, and Shukla was made to sit there. She looked beautiful with her long hair open in all its glory. She had peach-coloured flowers on her head, hands and feet. Her uncles, aunts and cousins came one by one and put the turmeric paste on her hands, feet and face. The turmeric gives an amazing glow to the skin. This is also one of the reasons turmeric is applied to brides and grooms. Her friends laughingly put the turmeric daintily on her face, her feet and hands. The same ritual was also taking place in Dhan Singh’s house. But the same rituals were being done so very differently there. Dhan Singh was sitting in his dhoti and vest while all the cousins were putting the turmeric paste all over him. His vest had already been torn and now the cousins were trying to get at the dhoti. But Draupadi’s stern voice reached out to them, “Enough is enough.”

“Let him go and have a bath. He has a long evening ahead!”

The party broke up and Dhan Singh went to take a bath in peace.

In the evening, there was panic. The band who played dholki and trumpets and would usher the groom had not reached. The baraat was getting late. Dhan Singh hated being late. He berated his brothers, “You should have told them to come two hours before the function!” Everyone was trying to figure out what to do next as Dhan Singh was pacing up and down the pathway.

Bikram was wondering if he should go and try to get another band, but he knew it was too late. Thankfully, a sudden commotion outside signalled that the band had arrived. Everyone heaved a sigh of relief. Now, they could proceed to the bride's house. The panditji was ushered in, and he began the ritual. Dhan Singh sat on the horse with one of his little nephews.

Dhan Singh was missing his own horse. He loved horses. He had bought a horse and had named him Toofan, which he took riding every morning. It had been very convenient for him to have a horse. The bachelor's rooms were close to his mess. There were stables in the mess, and Toofan was well looked after in those stables. But now that he was getting married and would be living in the married quarters, it was going to be difficult for him to take care of Toofan.

So he had given Toofan to a young officer who loved horses the way he did, and he would take care of him the way he had done. This way, he had access to Toofan without having to be responsible for him.

All the relatives, young and old, and the little children danced to the tunes of the band. The baraat soon reached Shukla's house, which was not even a kilometre away. The ceremony of entering the bride's house is called *janti aagman*. Her father, Har Bahadur Singh Thapa, and brother, Shankar Thapa, along with the other relatives, came to receive them. Her father put his handkerchief on the ground and then picked up the groom from the horse and put him on that handkerchief. This was a sign of respect given to the son-in-law. The bride's father then put a red tika on the groom's forehead, welcoming him. At the same time, Shukla entered wearing a beige saree, and the entry of the bride is called *kanya aagman*. She was wearing beautiful gold jewellery and a gorgeous round nose ring. A red bindi adorned her forehead with tiny bindis above her eyebrows. Her lips had been painted in deep red, and her hair was in one plait. She looked beautiful. Her face was almost completely covered by a red net dupatta. She was carrying a garland of roses, which, amidst the panditji's chanting, she put around Dhan Singh's neck. He did the same, all the time trying to look at her face, which was hidden.

Once the swayamvar was done, they then proceeded to the special chairs where they sat, waiting for the panditji, who called them shortly. Small cushions had been put for them at the marriage mandap so that the bride, groom, panditji and parents could sit in comfort.

Shukla's parents took her right hand and put it in the groom's right hand, reciting sacred verses, thus entrusting their daughter to the groom in this ceremony called *hast milap*. Shukla had no idea what was happening. She was too nervous, stepping into a new life. She looked at her father with her doe-like eyes, where there was already a film of tears. She was blindly following what he and the panditji kept telling her to do. Panditji started the havan. In the fire box some small pieces of wood were placed and he lit up that wood and put desi ghee to keep the fire going. He chanted his holy verses as they kept putting *samagri* in the havan kund.

The bride and the groom prayed to the Agni god by lighting the fire to witness their commitment to each other. Before starting the *saat pheras*, the pallu was tied to the scarf which the groom carried around his neck.

This is called *lagaan gathon* and indicates their bond that starts with this wedding knot. Then start the seven circumambulations around the havan kund. Shankar held the pallu and the bridegroom's scarf, making sure that all the customs were carried out seamlessly. The smoke from the havan was hurting Shukla's eyes, but she dared not rub them. The seven pheras symbolize a prayer of nourishment, strength, prosperity, family, progeny, health, love and friendship. This was followed by the *sindoor daan,* where Dhan Singh put sindoor in the parting of his bride's hair. As he lifted the veil covering her face, he was surprised to see the sheen of tears in her eyes. He wanted to gather her in his arms but controlled himself. Consoling himself that most brides cry on their wedding day, he put the sindoor on Shukla's *maang.*

Dhan Singh then took out a necklace made of *pote* (shiny glass beads) and *tilhari* (a gold piece) necklace, and put it around Shukla's neck. Pote necklaces were worn only by married women. Dhan Singh and Shukla were finally married.

There was a sudden shower of flowers on them. The couple then got up and, with Dhan Singh leading the way, went to his mother and bent down to touch her feet. Draupadi blessed them and enclosed both of them in her arms. Then they went to Shukla's parents, touched their feet and received their blessings.

"You must be tired!" whispered Dhan Singh. Shukla shyly nodded. More than shy, she was a little nervous. Starting a new life that day with people she hardly knew. But this was the way of life.

After touching the feet of almost all the elders, they finally sat down on their own special chairs. The brothers were instructed to get food for them. Before long, everyone had eaten dinner, and it was time to go.

Shukla's father hugged her tightly. This was bidai time, when the bride leaves for the groom's house after all the functions are over. All her relatives, aunts, uncles and cousins came forward to hug her. Everybody was in tears. Dhan Singh was getting very impatient. He gently pulled her towards the car which was going to take them home. The car was a very famous Dodge car that had been bought by Dhan Singh and three of his Army friends. They had invested a lot of money in it, and all of them took turns driving and retaining ownership of the car. The car was decked up with flowers to take Shukla to her new house. She hugged her father and, seeing tears in his eyes, began to sob. She could not hold her tears back any longer.

Trying to sob silently, she let the silent tears roll down her cheeks. Seeing Shankar cry upset her as well. She had always thought he would be a great support for her dad. But now, looking at him sobbing, she was totally undone. She kept thinking about who was going to take care of them.

Looking back to take a last look at the house, she spotted her helper crying as well. This triggered a fresh bout of tears. Kajal or no kajal, the tears would not stop.

Eventually, she sat in the car, crying with Dhan Singh gently holding her hand. In two minutes, they were in the house where all of them were staying. Here, the excitement palpitated as a host of relatives were waiting to welcome them. Soon, they were all laughing and joking and pulling the newlyweds' legs. Children would come, again and again, peer under her dupatta to take a look at her. Dhan Singh came down and told them that she was tired and to let her go and rest. Her sister-in-law Shakuntala came to help her to her room and told her to rest in a very mischievous tone. She sat quietly on the bed waiting for her groom as she had seen in innumerable Hindi films, but she was so tired that before she knew it, she fell fast asleep.

The next day, she woke up a little late. She had a bath, changed into a pink saree and wore matching bangles. Very shyly, she put the vermillion powder in the parting of her hair. Today, according to tradition, she would go back to her father's house. Dhan Singh and his relatives would accompany her. She and her husband would spend the night there. Dhan Singh took one look at her and thought she was truly beautiful. And at this moment, he wholeheartedly agreed with whoever had said that beauty was not in the face but that beauty was a light in the heart. He shrugged and came back to the real world. "Let's go," he told her. He was a stickler for being on time and would rather be five minutes early than be five minutes late.

Downstairs, Draupadi was doing puja and signalled to them to sit down. Shukla was in a daze with so many new customs and rituals, as well as so many new relatives. There were so many feet to be touched. Though she was expecting this, it still didn't stop her heart from beating fast whenever she thought she had made a mistake.

They were going back to her house for lunch. She was looking forward to seeing the familiar faces of her father and brother, as well as her aunts and uncles.

Her father and brother, along with the other relatives, came out and welcomed them when they reached, applying tikas on their foreheads. Draupadi and her relatives reciprocated the act for Har Bahadur Thapa's family. They also gave each other gifts. This was followed by a lavish lunch. Having reached home, seeing familiar faces and having finished the biggest ritual of her life, she finally relaxed.

First things first, she called Shankar and told him, "Go get me a plateful of food."

Chuckling, he told her, "Didi, today is a sit-down lunch, so you get to sit with your husband and eat as much as you wish."

Soon, everyone was seated at their tables, and the waiters began serving them. Shukla dug into her food like no one's business. By the time she was finished, her plate was full of chicken bones.

Her husband looked at her plate and smiled naughtily, "Poor chicken, today was not that chicken's day!"

Shukla blushed deep red and pretended she hadn't heard him. She concentrated on the dessert instead.

Lunch was soon over and it was time for all the relatives from the groom's side to go back. Dhan Singh would stay back with Shukla and would return the next day. Again, the whole routine of touching everyone's feet ensued before they were left on their own. Shukla went to her room to pack a few more things she had forgotten to take.

Dhan Singh followed her, "Can I help you?"

"No, you go and sit with Pitaji. I will join you in some time," she said.

But Dhan Singh reclined on the bed and said, "I have eaten too much. My stomach is bursting. I am going to rest for five minutes, and then I will go sit with the family." Even before she finished her packing, she turned to look at her husband. He was fast asleep. Putting a light cover on him, she tip-toed out of the room.

Everybody was sitting in the garden and having tea. She told the helper to get her a cup of tea as well. Her father told her to sit next to him, "All well?" he queried.

She coyly nodded her head, "They are very nice people. Very warm and caring."

"You take care of them. Draupadi has been taking care of all of them. Now it's your turn."

Having said that, he went back into the house as he had dinner to arrange.

There were still many relatives in the house. They would all be leaving in a day or two. Dinner was special that night as his *jawai* was present.

It was the 7th of May, 1955, the second day after the wedding. Yet there were so many rituals to complete. Shukla, with her husband, father and relatives, would go to her husband's house on the second day. She was dressed in a bright pink sari, and was a little less shy and nervous.

In the other house, everybody was singing and dancing. The mood was festive as they waited for their special guests to arrive. A special dinner was arranged, which was a good way for the family to get to know each other. Shankar was having a good time. He was a guest and the bride's brother, so he didn't have to do any running around. He was being looked after, and yes, he made sure he was well looked after. But he kept well away from his sister. He knew she could tear his image to smithereens in a minute. And here he had to maintain his image as he had spied two pretty cousins of Dhan Singh whom he wanted to impress.

The next day was going to be a tough day. Shukla had to prepare food for her newly acquired relatives. So she got up early, quickly took a bath, and completed her puja. She made her way to the kitchen. She decided to wear a yellow saree, specially presented to her by Draupadi for this day. She wore a matching bindi and bangles, her bangles making a sweet jingling noise.

Nervously, she entered the kitchen, ready to make lunch, but the cooks had already made the lunch. Draupadi was already there, busy overseeing them. She smiled tenderly and said, "Don't worry, lunch is made. You just have to make puris for everyone. You'll have time to do lunches and dinners later!"

Smiling at her mother-in-law, she started to fry the puris. By the time lunch was over, it was time for dinner. But she could relax as they were not expecting her to cook. She had to finish her packing. She quickly sneaked to her room to pack. She had just finished packing when her husband walked in.

"Have you done my packing as well?" surprised he asked her.

She nodded and smiled.

"Do you want to go to Kulu Manali for our honeymoon? But we really don't have time. I want to take you to Shimla for two days and show you all my favourite haunts. Then Solan for a few days and then back to my unit. I really don't know how to fit in Kulu Manali in between."

Dhan Singh had been talking to her about going to Kulu for their honeymoon, but they were going to Shimla for a few days first and then Solan. He also had to rejoin his unit soon.

"I am happy to go to Shimla and Solan," Shukla said shyly. So it was decided that Shimla and Solan it would be.

Chapter 16

The Journey Starts

The New Journey Begins..

Shukla was enjoying the car ride to Shimla with the rest of the family. The winds were trying their best to entangle her neatly combed hair, but the breeze seemed pleasant on her face.

The rest of the family was talking about the wedding, how they all had enjoyed it, and how it would take a few days to recover from the excitement. They were all tired, and though they would miss the excitement of the wedding lunches and dinners, they were quite happy to get back to their routine.

Everyone had plans of not getting up from their beds for two days at least. Not that it would actually happen, but you don't have to pay for dreams, so there is no harm in dreaming.

Draupadi was telling Dhan Singh that her brother had designated a special room for him and his bride for the two days they were going to be there. He smiled thinking it would have been more fun to share a scrap of childhood with Shukla with all of them sleeping in the childhood room, fighting, screaming, shouting.

But he did not suggest it, for he knew that having been the only girl in her family she was used to her privacy and being on her own.

He gave her a look sideways, "Charming," he said to himself.

The mischievous wind had decided to play with her hair once again, pushing the tendrils out of her plaited hair. Shukla was enjoying the cool, frivolous breeze on her face so much that she had stuck her entire face out of the window.

Draupadi said, "Please put your face inside; you might get hurt!"

Shukla said, embarrassed, "Ji."

A little upset at being told off in front of the family, her ready tears were raring to go. But she took a deep breath and was more than okay when she felt Dhan Singh's hand catch hold of one of hers and hold it gently.

The rest of the family was coming to Shimla on a bus from Joginder Nagar. Shimla was about two hundred kilometres away, and it would take them around seven hours to reach.

They were planning to stop halfway and have some tea. They spied a little roadside café, and everyone shouted in unison, "Stop!"

They were a little tired, and wanted to stretch their legs. They stopped at Sundernagar, a small sleepy little town halfway to Shimla. Shukla was getting tired and this was a welcome break. They had a bit of tea and ordered some lunch. Everyone wanted to have some dal and rice. The simplicity of the food after the rich food of the wedding was much appreciated.

Shukla and Dhan Singh went for a short walk to stretch their legs, enjoying each other's company and the beauty of the hills. Shukla sighed. She was happy as her husband was someone she had always dreamt about. She could sense his immense love for her and she felt warm and secure basking in the warmth of that love. They would have gone on walking but the rest of them started calling to them.

Soon they were on their way as they wanted to reach before dark. In Shimla, a warm home awaited them. Their aunt had come back a day earlier with one of the sons. They had hot dinner and a warm house all ready for them. Their rooms were also ready.

Dinner was served in the dining room. It was a room that was converted into a bedroom for the children after the meals were over. Mamiji had gone out of her way to make a special dinner for them. There was dal, aloo ka achar and mutton with rice. Huge containers of food were placed in the dining room, and then there was a scramble for the food. Before one could say 'Jack Robinson, ' the food was finished. After years of experience, his Mami had learned to serve the elders first and then let the kids eat. She had served Shukla as well, knowing she would not be able to cope with the scramble.

Luckily, Shukla got a second helping. Their Mami had saved it for her. Shukla looked at her food and looked guiltily around, with all the cousins looking enviously at her. But she quickly learnt the art of gobbling down the food before her guilty conscience took over!

The next morning, Dhan Singh wanted to take Shukla around Shimla and show her his school and the football grounds, take her shopping and go out for lunch. So excitedly, he walked into the kitchen for breakfast and told Shukla to get ready.

"Are you ready?" he asked her.

She was surrounded by his brothers and cousins.

"Ready, yes. Where are we going?"

And then she looked at all the cousins who were all ready to go with them.

Very disappointedly, he looked at her and said, "I thought we would go out."

Shukla was dying to laugh. She could guess he wanted to take only her with him, but he was in a fix.

He was very disappointed as he had wanted this to be a special day, but he relaxed and thought, I have a lifetime with her.

He shouted, "Okay, everyone, let's go!"

There was a sudden rush as everyone quickly got up, looking for their jackets and mufflers.

But Draupadi's strident voice stopped them all. "No one is going anywhere. Let the newlyweds go. All of you have chores to complete. Please finish them."

Not a word was said, but their expressions said it all. Disgruntled, in slow motion, they removed their shoes, their jackets, and mufflers. Dhan Singh felt bad, but in his heart of hearts, he thanked his mother. What a lady she was. She could control an army!

Very excitedly, Shukla wore her most comfortable chappals because he had told her that it was going to be a long walk.

Dressed in her favourite blue saree with a big bindi on her forehead and matching blue glass bangles on her hands, she was raring to go. But she had to run to catch up with Dhan Singh. He immediately slowed down when he realized he was too fast for her. They walked to his school. He showed her the tree where he used to hang his football shoes; then he showed her the football ground where he had had many earth-shattering moments. Then they just walked around chatting and looking for a place to have lunch.

Finally they found this restaurant which said that their specialty was chicken. Laughing, they decided to look no further and went in.

Ordering a huge lunch and their special chicken curry for her, he asked her, "Is this okay or do I need to order something else?"

He knew she loved chicken, so they had a huge meal with lentils, beans, rice and chicken. The special chicken came floating in oil, the beans were red in colour, and the dal looked interesting with one green chilli floating on top. But they were so hungry they relished it all. The fresh, cold air and the long walk had stimulated their appetite.

Shukla enjoyed the oily chicken immensely, licking the oil off her fingers. She told Dhan Singh, "I will become fat like a ball if I keep eating like this."

"Football or tennis ball? I love balls."

Dhan Singh as was his habit finished all the dishes. There was not a morsel left by the time he finished. They decided to skip the dessert.

After their meal, they chatted in one of the innumerable hawa ghars of Shimla.

Sitting on those uncomfortable wooden benches, they looked at the sky changing colours from light blue to a fluorescent peach as the evening approached. Shukla looked at Dhan Singh very seriously and said, "I want lots of children, and I have even thought of the name of my firstborn. She will be named Pamela."

Dhan Singh replied, "How do you know the baby will be a girl?"

"I just know!" replied Shukla.

They decided to walk along the very famous Mall Road of Shimla. This was a very popular road which the tourists frequented. There were a lot of shops on this road. Not only shops, it had the offices of the municipal corporation, fire service and the police headquarters as well.

Both of them strolled lazily, looking at the shops. They were just happy being with each other. He saw a lovely red coat hanging in one of the shops. He wanted to buy it for his wife, and it seemed like the perfect gift.

They went into the shop, and she tried it on. It fitted her beautifully.

"I love it!" said Shukla as the shopkeeper packed it. It was her first gift from him.

Below the Mall Road, there were lower bazaar streets connected by a number of steep steps. These bazaars were always very crowded. You got almost everything here, from stationery, spices, shoes, clothes, vegetables, meat and confectionery. This was an ideal place to buy gifts for everybody at home. And that's what this couple did. Then they trudged up and down the road carrying huge packets.

From Mall Road, they went to Kali Bari temple to pay their obeisance before heading home. They reached home pleasantly tired with small gifts for everyone. There was a lot of noise and laughter as they opened their gifts. The next day, everybody decided to go with them to the Jakhu temple and this time, Draupadi didn't dissuade them. Since the day after they would be going to Solan, it was more than understood that they would all be together on that day.

Jakhu temple is Lord Hanuman's temple and is quite famous. According to Ramayana, in the battle between Ram and Ravan, a very powerful arrow hit Lakshman, and nothing could revive him. Then, a very well-known priest told Lord Rama that only the

Sanjivini herb would help Lakshman. So Hanuman ji was sent to get it. On his way, Hanuman Ji stopped and met Sage Yaako while searching for the herb to revive Lakshman. He promised to meet the learned sage on his way back to Lanka. But Hanuman ji, in his hurry to get the herb for Lakshman, could not stop to meet the sage. So the sage was disappointed, but they say that as Hanuman Ji left this place, his idol emerged on its own. Yaakov then made the Jakhu temple to honour Hanuman Ji. It is believed that this temple has its footprints. Later, in 2010, a huge 108-foot-long idol was built, which has become one of the main attractions of Shimla.

They walked to the temple from the old bus station in Shimla. It was an hour's walk to the temple. Since it was Hanuman Ji's temple, there were a lot of monkeys around. The monkeys were believed to be Hanumanji's descendants. Shukla was not scared. She had a lot of protectors around her.

Her husband was gently holding her hand and after every ten minutes, he would ask her if she was okay and she would nod, "Yes, I'm fine."

They walked a good amount, but it seemed like nothing because walking amidst lush greenery along those winding trails was truly pleasant. Dhan Singh was worrying about her as it was a long walk. All of them were used to it, but he was sure Shukla did not walk as much as they all did. It was only much later in his life he realized that she was a woman of substance, not much scared or deterred by anything.

She, in his existence, became an anchor as do most Army wives. They are left alone in the Army cantonments when the husbands go to the field. They learn to cope, and most importantly, become independent women of conviction.

Chapter 17

The Army Wife

It takes a strong person to be a soldier. It takes a stronger person to love a soldier.

— Sarah Moore

Dhan Singh was posted to Mathura, so they started their married life in Mathura Cantonment. They were allotted a typical Army house, which had been built years ago. But it had a small garden in front and a vegetable garden at the back. It was an old British house, and he was looking forward to living a normal married life there with Shukla. She loved the house. It was hers and his, her own piece of heaven. She pranced around the house and was delighted with the garden.

Being very fond of plants, she was looking forward to planting various flowers and different kinds of plants in the front garden. The gate of the house was a little squeaky and it was almost falling apart.

Dhan Singh said, "Don't worry, I will get it fixed."

"I want it painted white as well!" she added.

The orderly had tried to get the house cleaned and it was looking quite neat. He had made an effort and put some flowers in an old vase he had found. He had even got lunch for them in a tiffin carrier from the mess. Dinner was to be hosted in the mess by the Commanding Officer (CO). It was like a small reception for the newly married couple.

For Shukla, all this was so new. She had never even attended a semi-formal party, and here, there was a special Army formal black-tie reception for her. She was in a quandary, and she didn't know what to wear. She had no idea how these Army parties functioned.

She called out to Dhan Singh, "What should I wear?"

Unpacking her trunk, she took out a bright red saree and asked, "Is this fine?"

"No, not this; show me some more!"

He chose a pale pink saree with golden embroidery and said, "You'll look beautiful in this!"

Shukla was young and very nervous at having to face the sophisticated senior Army wives. But when she met them, she found them to be warm and caring. She was greeted and congratulated by all the officers of the unit.

Dhan Singh introduced her to the seniors and the juniors. He felt as proud as a peacock, guiding her to the dining room. He made her sit next to the CO's wife.

She was asked a lot of questions by the other Army wives as to where she was from, about her parents, and what she liked doing. Quite like an Army interview, she thought.

She was really impressed with the whole atmosphere. The dining room was grand and the bearers were all dressed in crisp white clothes, and the chandeliers were gleaming. In fact, the brightly-lit room and her own nervousness were beginning to give her a headache.

Opposite her sat her handsome husband. Looking at the array of cutlery next to her plate, she was confused as to what cutlery she should use. She peeked at what Dhan Singh was using. Seeing him pick up the fork, she did the same. Then she saw him pick up the spoon, and she picked up the spoon and tried to eat the lentils and rice with her fork and spoon. But she wasn't able to, so she just gave up and used the fork. She did not even attempt to eat the chicken, her favourite. The dessert – the fruit trifle was wonderful. She managed a double helping of that, despite the fact that everyone had finished and they were just waiting for her. After dessert, the men went to smoke and have their liquor at the bar. The wives went to the lounge. They sat chatting about their children, school, and new recipes. When they learned that she could sing and play the sitar as well, they all got after her to sing. Shukla was too shy. She just sat wishing that the earth would open up and she could miraculously disappear.

Despite her continuous 'no', they kept asking her to sing. In walked her hero and he sat down next to her. She felt safe with him.

Then the request came from the CO's wife, "I would love to hear your lovely wife sing!"

"I am right here, so I would really be proud if you could sing for me," said Dhan Singh softly.

Everyone started clapping and abruptly stopped as soon as Shukla started to sing. She sang the popular song from the movie *Mr and Mrs 55* which had just released that February. The song was, '*Thandi hawa kaali ghata*'.

A shy, beautiful Shukla with her pale pink bindi singing like a star made the atmosphere magical. After she finished, they just couldn't stop clapping. If she had her way, she would have hidden her face in Dhan Singh's shoulder and would have refused to look up. But that was not possible. It would have embarrassed him thoroughly. So she sat there blushing and thanking everyone for their compliments.

The party broke up soon. The CO's wife invited them for dinner at her house the next day. Shukla's heart sank. Not another formal dinner, she thought.

On Monday morning, the normal routine of their life started. Shukla started learning the ropes of being an Army wife. Dhan Singh would go off early morning for PT (physical training), come home and change into his uniform. He'd then go to office. Then, he would be home for lunch. He looked forward to lunch at home as he was treated to Shukla's fine cooking.

After resting for an hour, he would go for games in the evening. He would wear his white shorts and white t-shirt, and off he would go for his game sessions. Football was such a passion with him, it naturally continued in the Army as well.

Every evening there were football matches where the officers and the jawans who played well, played together. He would come back home after the games, take a shower and they would sit and have tea together. They had begun living a life full of happiness and contentment.

One morning, Shukla woke up not feeling like herself. Since this morning, she has not been feeling very well. She wanted to throw up and was wondering what she had eaten the previous night. And that morning of all mornings, the senior wives were coming for a cup of coffee and a chat. She had especially arranged snacks and coffee for them.

One of the ladies asked, "Are you enjoying yourself here?"

Shukla replied, "I like it here, and all of you make it special. It's true you all have helped me so much to adjust to Army life; otherwise, living alone without any family around would not have been easy!"

They were all happy to hear this. Mrs Mona, who had got posted out and was going to Bangalore was saying, "Now I have to start packing. The children have to be taken out of school and I have to get their leave certificates. A new school for them. A new city and a new house for me!"

The CO's wife commented, "You can go to South India or to North India, the Army cantonment areas pan India look the same. There will be very well-maintained roads, well- manicured-gardens and freshly-painted white stripes on the sidewalks."

Suddenly Shukla got up as she began feeling nauseous. She went to the bathroom and vomited all that she had eaten. As she was gone for more than ten minutes, Mrs Mona, who had become her mentor came to the room to ask her, "Are you okay?"

Shukla, looking pale, told her, "I haven't been feeling too well. I have been nauseous all morning. I don't know what I ate last night."

Mrs Mona chuckled, "You go to the gynaecologist. Maybe you are pregnant. But no need to announce it just as yet till it's confirmed!"

After the ladies left, she lay down feeling drained.

In the afternoon when Dhan Singh came home to have lunch, she said, "I have something to tell you!"

He said, "Even I have to tell you something, but you tell me first!"

She smiled. " I think I'm pregnant, but I will only know for sure tomorrow after I get a check-up at the gynaecologist's!"

Dhan Singh got up in the middle of his lunch. He was elated.

"I'm sure you are pregnant!" he said as he kissed her stomach.

He went to the little room which had been converted into a small temple. He thanked God and asked Him to bless them.

After their prayers, they sat down to finish lunch. "Now, your turn, tell me your news," said Shukla.

"Get ready," he says. "Our daughter is going to be born in Jammu. I am getting posted to Jammu. Exciting, isn't it? New places to explore, new places to see!"

She replied, "But I have just settled down here. I have made friends. Now, I will have to start all over again. And the packing... to pack all of this?"

She looked around at the house. "And my plants?" she added. "What will happen to them?"

"I will help you, Kedu," he said, calling her by the short form of her second name, Kedari.

Dhan Singh was happy with his posting to Jammu. It had a decent hospital. And now that Shukla would be expecting a baby, a good hospital was a definite requirement.

The next morning, Dhan Singh took her to the military hospital. There was a long queue of pregnant women waiting for their check-ups. Dhan Singh was not at all embarrassed at being the only man there with his wife. Handling her as though she was made of Dresden China, he patiently waited for their turn.

And when they finally went in, he was very excited and asked the doctor, "Is she fine?" After the check-up, he anxiously asked, "Is she pregnant?"

The doctor confirmed that she was indeed pregnant, and he was ecstatic. Once they were back home, he made her lie down and told her she had to rest now.

And that he would make lunch.

"I have already made lunch!" laughed Shukla. "I am pregnant, not sick!"

But nothing doing, he warmed their lunch and laid the table. "I'm calling Mataji to Mathura. Someone should be with you!" he said as they had lunch. Shukla gave up and started to enjoy his pampering.

After lunch, he tucked her in bed and told her, "Don't worry about dinner. We will get some food from the mess."

But as soon as he left, Shukla got up. She was not the kind to keep lying down for no rhyme or reason. There was so much to be done. They had to start packing. They had to plan their packing. Now, with this little baby coming, she really had to go slow. She was very happy because Dhan Singh was happy. She prayed to God to let them always stay this happy.

Chapter 18

JAMMU AND NAGALAND

> Military spouses are the rock on which their families, our military community and our national security depend.
>
> —Joe Biden

They had arrived in Jammu. Shukla got busy unpacking and making a home of a house.

By now, she had a big stomach, and her pregnancy was a good excuse not to attend the formal dinners hosted in the mess. She was actually quite uncomfortable, and then there always seemed like a mountain of work to be done at home.

Her mother-in-law was unable to come to Jammu. There was a lot happening on the farm, and she couldn't leave Solan yet. Dhan Singh did not want her to go to her father's house in Joginder Nagar as there were no good hospitals there. So, to stay put in Jammu was a better idea. Shukla was admitted to the hospital on 2nd March 1956. On 3rd March, a beautiful baby girl was born. She was a skinny little baby and looked like a delicate doll. Dhan Singh was over the moon. He had always wanted a girl and this pretty little thing had clasped his heart in her two little hands.

Shukla had arranged everything before she left for the hospital. The baby's crib in the room and her clothes and diapers were in their cupboard. She had sterlized the baby's milk bottles and had shown Dhan Singh how to make the baby's formula and wash the bottles. The first few days were tough at home, but not unmanageable. He loved it when he fed the baby with the bottle and she in turn held his fingers in her small little hands. It was a matter of a few days. With Shukla growing stronger each day, she started to take over. After that, it was only playtime for Dhan Singh and the baby. The rest was handled by the baby's mother. They named her Pamela as they had decided. Shukla was enjoying being Pamela's mother. It was like she had acquired a little doll. She enjoyed dressing her up in cute dresses which she stitched herself. She made different kinds of baby food for her as she grew older and she became enamored by this little baby.

For Dhan Singh, too, this little human was like a new toy. He was enjoying every gurgle, every cry, and every laugh of hers.

But then, time moved on. Soon, another transfer order came through. He had been posted to Mokukchung in Nagaland. Again, there was a lot of packing to do. The years added more things to be packed. Nagaland was a tough posting. There was a lot of insurgency and inter-ethnic conflicts. After Independence in 1947, the area remained part of the province of Assam. There were numerous violent incidents that led to a lot of damage to civil infrastructure and to human lives.

In 1955, the Indian Army was sent to restore peace and order. In 1957, the Indian government and Naga leaders decided to make Naga Hills Tuensang Area (NHTA) a union territory to be administered by the Central government. Many tribes did not welcome this decision, so there was agitation and violence across the state. It was during this period Captain Thapa (Lieutenant Thapa had been promoted to Captain) was posted there.

The Naga ethnic groups were up in arms against the local villages. This was a strategic region close to China, East Pakistan and Burma, and these countries were always looking for a chink in the armour.

The villagers especially respected Captain Dhan Singh for his courage and boldness. Most of the chiefs of these villages were very fond of him. One even offered his daughter's hand in marriage to him. He politely declined, saying he was already married. There was a lot of violence in Nagaland, with a lot of infighting as well. There was constant patrolling and raids and ambushes. This was the only way to control them.

Captain Thapa landed there in the midst of it all, but he managed very well. It was the aura that he had, the fact that he was quite fearless while dealing with them, or the fact that he, too, had Mongolian features like the locals that helped. Whatever it was, his word carried a lot of weight. He was always the one chosen to be the mediator between the Army and the local people. Shukla, meanwhile, was quite happy there and had settled down. She was expecting her second baby by then.

It was one evening when he had gone for a counter-insurgency operation that Shukla's labour pains started. The baby had decided to come a week early. All alone at home with a small daughter, she was very worried. Though they had arranged for a midwife to come and help her during an emergency, she was scared in case there was a complication. The midwife was called for, and she did her best to comfort and guide Shukla.

It was a terrifying time for Shukla. She was in agony and kept crying for Dhan Singh. She was constantly looking out of the window. Through the chink in the curtains, she could see the gate and kept watching out for him. She would see the eerie inky darkness all around and deserted serpentine roads. The shadows of the trees in the pale moonlight and the dense forest all around looked menacing.

She was used to the loneliness and the gloomy darkness. It had never scared her, but that night the pain was playing havoc with her imagination. She clutched the midwife's hands. She was glad to have her here. The midwife smiled at her encouragingly. Luckily her daughter Pamela was fast asleep, otherwise the situation would have scared the little girl. Her contractions had started in the evening and when the contractions got stronger and more frequent, she had called for the midwife.

Then she took a bath and took out clothes she could wear easily after the child's birth. She had also taken out the baby's clothes and given them to the midwife so that the baby could be cleaned and dressed. All that work had been done.

Then came the waiting period. Her water bag had broken, and she was feeling sick. Her back had really started to hurt.

The midwife held her gently and finally told her to push. After what seemed like an eternity, she felt the baby's head between her legs. And then, slowly, the baby appeared.

"It's a girl," said the midwife with a smile. She cut the umbilical cord and gently clamped it. She gave her to Shukla, who forgot all her pain and worries the minute she cradled the baby.

The midwife carried on with her job. She waited patiently for the placenta to be delivered. Meanwhile, the contractions were still going on, but they were very mild. The midwife cleaned her up and helped clean the baby. She told Shukla to try and breast feed the baby. Before long, mother and daughter were fast asleep.

The next morning, there was a lot of excitement around the house. Captain Thapa had been informed that his wife had delivered a baby, and he was due home any minute. Pamela was very happy with her baby sister. Every five minutes, she would come and touch her and say, “Mine?”

Shukla would laugh and nod, “Yes.”

Captain Thapa was delirious with happiness. Having grown up in a large family, he had wanted a big family of his own. He would gently hold the baby and feed the baby milk. He was quite good at it as he had learnt the tricks with his first born.

They named the baby Ramola, though everyone called her Golu. Golu looked like a fairy child. Soon after, they were posted to Dehradun. After the tense atmosphere in Nagaland, Dehradun was quiet and peaceful.

In Nagaland, Shukla had forever been stressed, always worrying about her husband. In Dehradun, she was relaxed. But it seemed she had relaxed too soon. Her beautiful daughter Ramola suddenly became unwell. Captain Thapa and Shukla rushed her to the Army hospital. The doctor examined the baby and gave her some medicines. He gave her an injection as well and told them to take her home.

They took her home, but her condition worsened, and that very day, she passed away.

Shukla and Captain Thapa were heartbroken. Ramola had been a beautiful child. Every time Shukla took her to the park in the pram, mothers and children would crowd around the baby, trying to touch her to see if she was real. She looked like a living doll.

After her sojourn in Nagaland and their daughter's passing, Shukla started clinging to Dhan Singh. She would tell him, "Promise me you will never leave me. I will never let you leave me."

It was a traumatic time for the family. There were so many memories of Ramola.

Shukla would be reduced to tears just looking at her toy or her milk bottle, things which Dhan Singh hadn't remembered to give away. In the nights, he cradled her like a child.

He knew it would be some time before her self-control and confidence would return. Death is so permanent, and the permanent bit was the scary part.

Death robs you completely. And when a mother loses her little child, it is the hardest thing to bear. Shukla became like a little child herself. Again and again, she would ask him to reassure her that he would be by her side forever. Pamela could not understand what had happened to her new sister. Every time she asked her mother where her sister was, her mother would hug her tightly and start crying.

But time is a great healer. Shukla became pregnant again. This time, they were close to a well-equipped hospital. On 17th August 1961, a baby girl was born. They named her Madhulika. This baby was very precious to them because they had had her after losing one baby to death. Regular life started with the same Army routine. Only it was school time for Pamela and pram time for Madhulika. Shukla remained busy with the children and the Army wives. They would sit and plan events and help the younger wives adjust to the Army way of life. They would learn to cook with and from each other.

If any jawan's wife had a problem, all of them got together to sort it out. They were like a big family and a huge support system. Since everyone was living on their own, they needed each other.

It wasn't till Shukla was pregnant with their third baby that Captain Thapa got a call.

Chapter 19

SIRIJAP

I promise... This is not a goodbye but a see you soon.

Captain Thapa was posted to Chushul. They had barely recovered from the nightmare of the death of their daughter and had started to live a normal life when the orders came in. Shukla wouldn't allow him to break the promise of leaving her alone when she was expecting another child. She had started to be happy again, even though a bit of her heart would always be dead and buried with the little child she had lost. With a heavy heart, he asked his CO if he could defer his posting.

"No, Thapa, you have to leave . You have been called because of your skills in the mountain terrain, diligence, sincerity and the excellent reports of your tenure in Nagaland posting," said his CO, but he promised him that once he got his replacement, he would be sent back.

He was asked to leave that very evening.

"I have to leave," he told Shukla.

"You promised me that you would be by my side, especially now. I need you; I need you with me. You promised," said a teary-eyed Shukla.

"I will be by your side all my life, but at this moment, my country needs me more. Duty calls; I need to be by my brother's soldiers," declared Captain Thapa solemnly.

Shukla kept quiet as she listened to him.

She had vaguely heard in the ladies' club, that rumours kept floating that the Chinese were everywhere along the Indo-China border where Captain Thapa was being posted. And that India was establishing forward posts in and around that area. She sighed and was wondering how she would cope. With two little daughters, herself heavily pregnant, and the constant stress about Dhan Singh, life would be tough.

Captain Thapa hugged her and said, "I will go and get you the highest gallantry award, the Param Vir Chakra for you. We will have a son named Paramdeep. I promise you, I will be back."

Shukla couldn't say anything after that. He just held both her hands and promised her, "I will be back!"

Turning towards his older daughter, he said, "I want you to look after your mother."

She nodded, understanding the need of the hour.

He hugged his daughters tightly. He went to the mandir room in the house and prayed to God. He prayed in gratitude for strength and prayed for victory. He prayed hard for Shukla.

She quickly went to the kitchen, took out some curd and mixed it with sugar. She knew it was supposed to be a good omen to put a tika and eat sweet curd. She put a tika on his forehead and fed him the sweet curd, praying all the while for his safety.

She was a forlorn figure with her two daughters, waving out to him as he was being driven away. Tears rolled down her eyes. She stood there till the jeep was totally out of sight. Then, clasping her two daughters, she came in. She was a tired figure wiping her tears. Her brain was telling her to stop crying in front of the girls and was also telling herself to be brave. She had to be brave for her Dhan Singh, for the little girls and for the baby in her womb.

The next day, it was a sad household that got up to bright sunshine and the chirping of the birds. Her elder daughter Pamela knew that her dad had gone to war so her mom was unhappy. She was sad, too, but she had to take care of her mother. Her dad had made her promise that she would look after her till he came back home.

She hugged her and said, "Mom, eat some food."

Shukla said, "No, later."

In the evening Shukla sat by the radio trying to listen to the news and to figure out what was happening. Both the daughters too realized that there was something amiss. They too would sit with her, glued to the radio, looking at her with sad, solemn eyes. They were watching her, fascinated at her restless fingers rotating the dial of the radio increasing and decreasing the volume. Her restless fingers caressed her womb, her restless soul in a quandary.

She fed her daughters listlessly, telling them, "Put on the news and don't touch the radio!"

She tried eating but ended up playing with the food on the plate and eventually gave up. She tried to get some sleep, but she could not sleep. She had to keep herself busy; otherwise, she would just worry relentlessly. Shukla was a no-nonsense Army wife. She would soon resume her duties and start looking after the house and the children. But that night, there was a certain restlessness about her, and it was wearing her out.

The 1st Battalion, 8th Gorkha Rifles, had set up the forward post Sirijap 1. The first battalion of the Gorkha Regiment was raised in the Anglo-Nepalese War in the year 1815. The British were so impressed by the valour displayed by the Gorkhas during the war that they started active recruitment of the Gorkhas in the British Indian Army. In 1947, after the Partition, six Gorkha regiments, 1st GR, 3rd GR, 4th, 5th, 8th and 9th GR, remained with the Indian Army while the 2nd GR, 6th GR, 7th GR, and 9th GR were transferred to the British Army. The 8th GR was raised in 1824, and this regiment fought in World War I and World War II. Since its independence, it has fought the Sino-India War of 1962 and the Indo-Pak War of 1971.

Captain Thapa reached Sirijap 1, which was located on the northern banks of Pangong lake of Ladakh. The post Sirijap 1 was a forward post established by the 1st battalion, 8 Gorkha Rifles. It was a part of the series of forward posts – a plan of the forward policy. A number of small posts were created facing the Chinese, and this plan was called the Forward Policy.

This was done to counter the increasing Chinese intrusions and their posts in Ladakh. There were constant skirmishes between the Indian and Chinese soldiers for control of the area between Pangong Tso and Spangur Tso. There would be a lot of talk on the loudspeakers, each telling the other to turn around and go back. The Chinese, being in larger numbers and with better equipment, were always at an advantage.

India never imagined that China would attack India, but tiny skirmishes had started to take place. China had started building posts around the posts that the Indian Army would build. But both the adversaries, though working around each other, did not fire at each other because both had instructions to fire only in defence.

On 11th September, it was decided all forward posts and patrols were to be given permission to fire on Chinese soldiers carrying firearms entering Indian territory.

Through the summer and autumn of 1962, a lot of military accidents and border clashes flared between India and China. The Indian Air Force was told not to plan air support, though at that point, looking at the Chinese soldiers' numbers, the Indian Air Force seemed the only feasible way to save a lot of uncalled-for deaths. The assumption that China would never attack did not let the Indian Army prepare for war with China, which resulted in the gigantic battalions of Chinese soldiers fighting with the minuscule battalions of Indian soldiers.

Captain Thapa was given command of the D company's 1st Battalion of the 8th Gorkhas, and he had to prepare this post for 48 square kilometres at Sirijap. And before he knew it, the Chinese had built posts on three sides of this post. Captain Thapa and his second in command (2IC), Subedar Min Bahadur Gurung, were dismayed to see how ill-equipped they were. He and his men were given the task of taking care of the post, but his soldiers did not even have proper clothes. They had no snow clothes and no proper boots to stay at such heights, let alone the equipment. What they had was totally obsolete in comparison to what the Chinese possessed.

He looked at them helplessly and thought to himself, 'God help them, and God help me!'

All the soldiers and he himself had been vigorously trained under the motto of service before self, so he began to make the best of the situation he was handed. He decided to take the challenge head on.

For him, no challenge was too difficult. He would make sure that he would give his all to save the honour of his country. He knew it could be at the cost of his life, but that thought never wavered his resolution. He had only twenty-eight soldiers to take charge of this post. Since forward posts were being established all over that area, and soldiers were being assigned to man them, that was the reason why there was a small number of soldiers assigned to each post.

He undertook the task knowing that they had to keep the Chinese out of Chushul and India. Chushul was 200 kilometres away from Leh. Chushul was the central point of the Sino-Indian War of 1962. There were two phases to the clashes in the Chushul sector, first at Sirijap on 20th October 1962 and then at Rezang La and Gurung Hill from 18th November onwards.

He knew the aim of the Chinese soldiers was to capture the Chushul airport. They were attacking from all sides to reach Chushul and take over the airport, which was the lifeline of the Indian Air Force in the area. To prevent this, 1/8th Gorkhas, 13 Kumaon, and 1 and 5 Jat were deployed in the area. Chushul lies at a strategic point as the road to the capital, Leh, passes through it. In October 1962, the work of Army engineers made the airstrip capable of flying a packet aircraft, a twin-engine cargo plane, and an AN-32 Soviet-made transport aircraft. The Chinese wanted control over Chushul for two main reasons – to cut off access to the capital, Leh, and to prevent any reinforcements coming in via the airfields, explains the official war history. [2]

Captain Thapa could make out that there were going to be tough times ahead, but he could see no option but to make the best of the situation. He figured that this was one of the important posts that had to stop the Chinese from making inroads into Chushul. He was constantly in touch with his battalion, communicating to them that the Chinese were building posts and surrounding these forward posts with posts of their own.

---

2 According to a report by *The Print*.

'This nation will remain the land of the free only so long as it is the home of the brave.' – Elmer Davis.

Remembering these words, Captain Thapa sighed. There really was no alternative but to make the best of the situation that had been thrust upon them. In the best Army tradition, he geared himself and his men to counter an impossible situation as they got busy organizing the forward post.

Every day, he would sit and talk to his men, encourage them, and organize the building of bunkers. It was a tough task to keep his soldiers' spirits high in this miserable situation. And a tougher job was to keep his own spirits high in the face of looming death. He knew that in any kind of war, the odds of death winning were always high, but there, surrounded by hundreds of Chinese soldiers, the probability of death was almost certain. Bravery was not all about fighting; it was also about facing death that was staring unblinkingly at your face.

The Chinese had built three posts around their single post. But sheer willpower kept him and his men going. His loyalty to his motherland commanded this. He could not and would not abandon this post for his life, but there were times he looked at his men and was overcome by the futility of it all. But he overcame these thoughts, knowing very well that there was no way out. So, he prepared his men to retaliate against the onslaught that was to follow.

Every day, he would talk and discuss ideas with his soldiers. They would abuse the Chinese and have a good laugh when the Chinese would come back with the 'Hindi Chini bhai bhai' retorts from a few yards away.

Dhan Singh sat on a boulder and rubbed his face with his hands. He did this every time he was stressed. It was a bitterly cold day. In October, Sirijap freezes to a lower than a minus degree temperature. He could feel the soft, feathery touch of the snow on his face before it slid down to the ground. He could feel the temperature dropping below freezing point as well as sense the ominous silence of the great mountains around him. He could feel eyes looking at him, but he shrugged off the uneasy feeling. He looked with great pride at all his men trying to organize this forward post. He thought to himself that if they did not die from made-in-China bullets, they would definitely die of the cold.

Calling his mess Havaldar, he told him, "Just make sure that you give us a lot of hot broth and good food."

"Okay, sir!"

That day was going to be a good day, thought Captain Thapa. He had got up with a very happy feeling. Sitting in his bunker, he sipped his extra sweet tea. The extra sweetness always rejuvenated him, and he enjoyed these few pleasures immensely.

His orderly got a few letters. There was a letter from the Army headquarters granting him leave, telling him that his replacement was on his way and that he could leave right away.

He could not believe it. He wanted to scream, and he wanted to shout. He was so happy till reality struck him on his face. Life has its own course, and you work around it. He was destined to fight this war, and so he fought it.

Amidst all the confusion of the looming war, to be told that his leave had been sanctioned and was a miracle. Before coming to Sirijap, he had asked for leave because his wife was expecting their third child. He had promised his wife that he would be there by her side close to the time when the baby was expected.

She had held his hand and made him promise. He could do nothing else, so he promised. He knew she was scared this time, having lost a baby to the clutches of death. Now, she was very insecure. She wanted him by her side, when she had this baby. So when he was informed that he could go on leave, he was happy that he could be at his wife's side during this time, but he was sad to leave the soldiers who had become like family to him in the past few days.

But realizing that his replacement had only reached Leh, Captain Thapa refused to leave the company headless till the replacement reached Sirijap.

His seniors, aware of his predicament, told him that he could leave as his replacement would be there in a day or two, but he refused. Ruefully looking at his wife's photograph, he said, "I am sorry, I am breaking my promise to you. But I will make up for all my broken promises if I survive!"

He knew to be able to survive this would be to survive just about anything in this world. He knew that he and his soldiers were unlikely to come out of this alive. He was free to go, but he chose to stay.

He rubbed his face with both his hands. At this point, he knew leaving his men would be disastrous. As it is they were sitting ducks for the Chinese soldiers. But if he went away, they would be like headless sitting ducks waiting to be massacred. He was also deeply involved in the defensive and for him to leave at this point was very difficult.

It's strange, but he was not even tempted to leave. He was that kind of a person. He knew this was his duty, and he had to perform. And perform he did!

He called out to Subedar Min Bahadur Gurung and pointed to the increased activity on the Chinese side. "What is happening? There is a lot of commotion!" he asked.

Captain Thapa could make out that something was cooking. It seemed like they were increasing their troops around Sirijap. He could see a lot of porters and a huge number of troops marching in with heavy weapons and guns.

Subedar Min Bahadur Gurung looked at Captain Thapa quizzically and said, "There is a problem."

"Are we ready?" asked Captain Thapa.

"We are okay."

'Yes, as good as we can be,' thought Captain Thapa.

He anticipated that an attack would be carried out soon. In fact, the Chinese troops had learnt one sentence, 'Hindi Chini bhai bhai', and they kept repeating that. It was to irritate the Indian soldiers, who would sometimes laugh at them and sometimes get worked up about it. Then, the Chinese would also keep repeating it and tell them to leave this area, saying it belonged to them.

Captain Thapa had been promoted to the rank of Major during the war. His ability to handle his men and the situation was always looked up to and applauded. Upon noticing the Chinese army making such advances, Major Thapa started to organize his troops. He increased the patrolling.

Standing on a huge boulder, he shouted to the soldiers, "Dig fast and dig deep!"

He got Subedar Min Bahadur Gurung to encourage his soldiers to talk to them.

This was the time when they needed all the mental and emotional support.

He also got the bunkers ready in good time. This was a huge task, considering they were on 6,000 metres high mountains with freezing winds and sub-zero temperatures and with no proper equipment and clothing for the soldiers. The ground was rocky and it was no mean task to break those rocks to make bunkers there. But they eventually used ration bags and sandbags to reinforce their defences. Even food was minimal.

But the Gorkhas, having lived in rough and tough conditions, were mentally and physically quite equipped to handle all of this.

On the night of 20th October 1962, the Chinese attacked the eastern sector of the Indian defences. That very same night, they attacked the posts at Galwan, Chip Chap and Pangong areas of Ladakh and across the McMahon line. The attack was a pretext for the disputed Himalayan borderline, but there were many more reasons. In 1959, after the Tibetan uprising, there had been a series of violent border incidents. And then, India granted asylum to the Dalai Lama, which, of course, irked the Chinese. Everything added up to lead to the war between India and China. India has always followed a policy of maintaining a cordial relationship with China. India was among the first few countries to grant diplomatic status to the People's Republic of China (PRC). India supported the demand for state recognition of the PRC. It also entered into negotiations with China on the question of Tibet entering into the Panchsheel Agreement in the year 1954. After Chou Enlai's visit to India in 1954, the Chinese started protesting against the presence of Indian soldiers in Brahoti, three kilometres south of a border pass, Tun Jun La, in Uttar Pradesh. Formally, this was the first time the Chinese had made any claims to Indian territory. The construction of the Tibet-Sinkiang Road in 1957 was a turning point in Sino-India relations as the Chinese occupied a large portion of Aksai Chin. Now, China had started to openly come up with territorial claims against India. By 1959, the Chinese soldiers had put up posts at Chushul, Rezang La, and Mandal just south of Dambu Guru. On 8th September 1962, Chinese troops encircled Dhola's post in the eastern sector and began firing. They launched similar attacks on the eastern Namku Chu sector, as well as the western sector in Ladakh.

There was an iron-clad synchronization in the Chinese army regarding these attacks. The entire assault was strategically planned and executed._They relied more on the principles of speed, surprise, and deception. And it seemed to work.

On 20th October 1962, early at 4:30 in the morning, the Chinese attacked Sirijap post 1.

Captain Thapa had been very uneasy all night; he kept getting up and going back to sleep. But eventually, he gave up. He picked up his heavy jacket, pulled up his boots and decided to take a round. The blistering cold wind was rebuking him and telling him to go back to the warmth of his bunker, but his mind refused to listen.

It was a dark night with the stars glittering. No clouds could be seen in the sky. Absolutely clear, it seemed as though the sky resonated with the light of the stars. He could see the mountains looming again in a most sinister way, trying to warn him of what lay ahead.

Suddenly, his eyes saw a trail of Chinese soldiers stealthily advancing towards him. Straight towards the post of Sirijap. He almost thought he was dreaming, seeing hundreds of Chinese soldiers making their way towards his post.

Quickly, he made his way to the guards and silently pointed towards those soldiers. He gestured for them to be quiet. Then, quietly, he woke up Subedar Min Bahadur Gurung, and then they woke up the rest of them. They waited till the Chinese soldiers were directly in front of them like walking ducks, and they could shoot them without much ado.

But the Chinese soldiers were huge in numbers. The Indian soldiers kept shooting, and many Chinese soldiers fell. But twice as many would take their place. They were like the rakshasa – one would fall, and twice as many would take their place.

But the Indian soldiers would not give up; they went on firing and fired till the guns became too hot for them to handle, and they had to drop the guns. They grabbed the guns of the dead soldiers lying around them. Some unsheathed their khukris and killed enemy soldiers with their bare hands. There was constant shelling of artillery and mortar fire from the Chinese side, giving covering fire to the Chinese soldiers who kept moving ahead. This allowed them to reach 150 yards to the rear of the post. The firing went on for what seemed like forever.

Suddenly, the artillery fire stopped. And then there was mayhem. Hundreds of Chinese soldiers moved forward, shrieking and screaming their war cry, moving ahead with great confidence, thinking it was going to be an easy walkover. However, they underestimated the strength and resilience of the Indian soldiers. They were confronted with the wrath of the dauntless Gorkhas.

"Jai Maa Kaali Ayo Gorkhali!" (Hail Goddess Kali, the Gorkhas are here) screamed the Gorkhas as they counter-attacked. The echo of the war cry resounding from the barren mountains chilled the bones of the ferocious Chinese soldiers. They replied with heavy artillery fire and mortar fire.

There was no stopping the oncoming Chinese soldiers. They were swarming like hundreds of ants crawling stealthily and steadily towards their prey. Captain Thapa commanded his soldiers to fire. They were unafraid, their bravery unequalled in the world. Looking at the hundreds of Chinese soldiers approaching them, they knew that eventually, they would all die, but before they died, they would kill as many as they could. It seemed like an endless black night. The Chinese were amazed that such a small army of soldiers was giving them such a tough fight. The Gorkhas fired their machine guns and their rifles, not one doubting the repercussions of it all. They lived up to the reputation of a Gorkha soldier and how! They killed and wounded the Chinese soldiers in colossal numbers, though it was not even a dent in the Chinese army numbers. On the contrary, the Indian troops suffered a lot of casualties. Each Gorkha soldier's death was an untold story of courage and valour.

More than a hundred Chinese soldiers were slowly approaching the hillside. Having seen the Gorkhas in action, they were being cautious. They had heard about the madness of the Gorkha's bravery. The whole world knew about it. That day, they were witnessing it. And this was making them vigilant. Having lost many men in the first attack, they were being careful the second time.

There was the incessant sound of firing from both sides, shattering the silence of that seemingly peaceful, silent night. The Chinese could not fathom what the Gorkha soldiers were made of. The strength of the Great Himalayas, these mighty mountains, was seeped into their blood.

Encouraging his soldiers, running from bunker to bunker, with bullets grazing past his shoulders, Major Thapa's adrenaline soared. There was no other thought in his mind except to save his soldiers, his country and his countrymen from the Chinese assault.

What other emotion except patriotism can give you so much madness in your courage that you fight and kill enemies with your bare hands? The khukris, which were twenty-inch curved swords, were used ferociously. According to tradition, every time they were unsheathed, they had to draw blood. These were used to fight the enemy mercilessly.

Major Thapa was protected by the gods themselves; otherwise, who could roll over a live grenade and still be alive? The Chinese were throwing incendiary bombs and grenades at the bunkers to smoke out the soldiers in and around the bunkers. Major Thapa saw one of the grenades close to one of his bunkers. To protect his fellow soldiers, he rolled over a live grenade, and before it could explode, he threw it back at the enemy, killing and wounding some of the Chinese soldiers. This was the madness of the very brave.

These soldiers wanted to protect every inch of their country. They descended on the Chinese like the cyclone wind; their fury unleashed, destroying anything and everything that came their way. They themselves suffered huge losses, but it was like they were on fire. They knew that they had to fight for their country, and they knew they had to fight for themselves. And they also knew that they were fighting against all odds. To make matters worse, their land communication link with the battalion was destroyed. Their wireless set was damaged, so they lost complete contact with the base.

Before the communication links of the company and the battalion were destroyed, Major Thapa could be heard by the Signal Battalion saying, "Don't worry, sir. I will defend my post... I will defend my country till my last breath!"

The last message was heard by Major Ved Vyas from the Signals Regiment. Major Thapa was declaring, "Neither will I withdraw, nor will I surrender." This was the last communication from Sirijap 1. After this, the communication system was blown apart, and nobody could connect with them.

Despite all this, the intense fighting went on. Having got rid of the grenade, he saw one of his soldiers getting shot in the arm. The gun fell from his hands as a result. The gun fell beyond the soldier's reach. Major Thapa rushed to the spot, picked up his rifle and gave it to him. He said, "Yes, we are all going to die, but let's not wait for death. Let's give death to them, and let's take the lot with us!"

Saying that he handed him the gun in the other uninjured hand. It seemed like an endless black night which was turning red with blood. The Chinese intensified the second attack. Now, they were just fifty yards away from the post. Major Dhan Singh told his soldiers, "We will take the bullets on our chest, never on our backs."

Dodging the Chinese bullets and grenades, Major Thapa and Subedar Min Bahadur Gurung went from bunker to post. They were here, they were there. They were everywhere to encourage the soldiers and to see if they were alright. And to check whether they were still armed.

Each one and every one of those dauntless Gorkhas fought till their last breath. Subedar Min Bahadur Singh collapsed under the debris of a bombed bunker, but in a few seconds, he emerged like a phoenix with his Light Machine Gun (LMG) and shot dozens of approaching Chinese soldiers. They, too, fired back at him, and he died after every part of his body was shot at.

Each and every Gorkha soldier of that post was a remarkable story of bravery and courage.

They suffered huge losses, but they were unstoppable. Even badly wounded soldiers kept on fighting till their last breath. One example was Naik Krishna Bahadur Thapa, who was hit by a splinter that severed his leg. Undaunted, he took over the LMG after the soldier who was manning it was killed. He started firing towards the advancing Chinese soldiers. He, too, was shot many times but didn't stop firing till his last breath.

After the second attack, there were only seven soldiers left to defend the Sirijap post. These seven Gorkhas knew that there was no way they were going to survive the onslaught, but now they were past caring. They were hungry for the blood of the Chinese soldiers. They wanted to avenge their fellow soldiers, whose warm blood they could still feel on their fingers as they had tried to stop their bleeding. The soldiers whose blood coated the entire area of Sirijap post 1. These Gorkhas were ravenous, and there was no stopping them. It was this hunger that made them give the Chinese soldiers a tough fight.

Major Thapa encouraged them, shouting, *"Kafir hunu bandha marno ramro!"* (Better to die than to be a coward!)

His face black, voice choked with smoke, and his attitude ferocious, he cried, "Let's give it to them if we have to die. Let's die fighting; let's die gloriously. Let's give them a fight they will not forget. A war that the world will not forget. Let each one of us kill as many as we can!"

And brandishing his khukri, he stepped out of his bunker.

The soldiers truly saw Maa Kali in him. It was like he had suddenly acquired four more arms, and he was killing the enemy soldiers with his khukri. His spirit was thirsting for their blood, and he was now unstoppable; his epinephrine at the highest. He himself was smeared with blood. He was hungry for revenge. He was ravenous for their blood, and he wanted each one of his comrades avenged. He was drunk with the fearlessness of death.

However, the third attack by the Chinese soldiers was the worst. They had suffered huge losses, and they wanted to wipe out the post completely. This third attack was brutal, where the Chinese used heavy machine guns and rocket launchers. This post was also being attacked from the side of the lake by an amphibious craft, and they were armed with heavy machine guns.

The Indian Army had almost run out of ammunition and were fighting with their bare hands. The khukris were their only weapons now. Heads rolled on the icy ground; blood flew in the air. There were slashes of frozen red blood on the white pristine ground. The Chinese were no less as they lobbied grenades at the Indian bunkers relentlessly.

Major Thapa looked around and saw how his men were being killed. His anger knew no bounds. He knifed every Chinese soldier with his khukri, not stopping nor caring that the gods of death were all around him. He only stopped when he saw the Indian bunkers burning. He knew that some of these bunkers had injured soldiers in them. And despite their injuries, they were firing with the LMGs from inside the bunkers.

Rushing to one of the flaming bunkers, he took an injured soldier from inside the bunker and dragged him outside. He was immediately surrounded by Chinese soldiers. One of them hit him with his rifle butt. They wanted to capture him alive. He heard a crack, and he could feel his front teeth break. Another Chinese soldier hit him on the head. He heard another crack and felt the blood oozing out from his head. A third Chinese soldier attacked him from behind, and that was the last crack Major Thapa heard and felt before he lost consciousness.

Three valiant Gorkhas survived this massacre. Two were taken prisoners, and the third, Rifleman Tulsiram Thapa, escaped and rejoined his battalion. Tulsiram recounted the bravery of these soldiers and of Major Thapa. He narrated how they had inflicted heavy casualties on the enemy and, despite all that, how Major Thapa had survived the rain of bullets and shelling of grenades. How picking up a live grenade to protect injured soldiers, he threw it back at the enemy. He told his seniors at the battalion how all of them had fought with extraordinary bravery.

Major Thapa was extremely proud of all of his thirty soldiers. Each one deserved a gallantry award, and more than that, they deserved their names written in golden letters. They were immortal. They never died and would live forever. A mere 30 men fought against hundreds of Chinese soldiers who were better prepared, better equipped and better clothed. The 30 soldiers went beyond the call of duty.

Zinda rehne ke mausam bahut hain magar.... jaan dene ki rut roz aati nahin.

***

Rifleman Tulsiram Thapa reached the battalion much later. Before that, there was no way the battalion headquarters could be informed of what was happening there. So, two storm boats were sent across the lake from the headquarters to find out what was happening in Sirijap.

Reaching the location, both the boats were fired upon by the Chinese. One of the boats capsized, and everyone who was on the boat drowned. They were quietly observing what was happening in Sirijap when the Chinese soldiers spotted them and started firing at them.

All the occupants of the first boat died. Naik Rabilal Thapa, who was in the second boat, escaped and returned to base. He had been sent by the battalion headquarters. He was sent to get information about what was happening there. The only place from where the Sirijap post could be observed was Thakung. This was used as a ferry point for the boats to maintain the post in the Pangong Tso area. Two boats were sent to Thakung and Naik Rabilal Thapa was in one of them.

He reported what he saw; he told them how bravely each and every soldier of the company was fighting and how these soldiers eventually fought with their bare hands with only their khukris. He talked about the unparalleled bravery of Major Dhan Singh Thapa. He narrated how he had seen him running from one soldier to another amongst the rain of bullets, how he had rolled over a live grenade to try and save the injured soldiers and throw the grenade back at the Chinese soldiers, how he had killed the Chinese soldiers with his khukri. How fearlessly he had fought with cool, conspicuous courage.

He saw the Sirijap post burn and reported that Sirijap was captured and all the soldiers were dead.

On the basis of these accounts and acknowledging the bravery of Major Thapa and his men, Major Thapa was awarded the highest gallantry award of the nation – the Param Vir Chakra – posthumously. He had fulfilled his promise to his wife and done his duty for the nation.

The Chinese were beaten back twice, and eventually, only three Gorkha soldiers were left. This did not deter Major Thapa.

He had continued to fight till he was captured in an unconscious state. The post was completely demolished and burnt down.

There were reports that in all the forward posts, jawans had bullet wounds on their chests. None of them had died with bullets on their back. They died with machine guns in their hands. Even the dead had machine guns clasped in their hands. Some of the soldiers in crouching positions, still with guns, had taken the bullets from the Chinese on their chests. This was the story of many soldiers posted across posts scattered over Chushul. If these posts had not put up a tough fight, the Chinese would have captured the Chushul airport and subsequently moved forward easily. But because these soldiers fought with so much valour, other posts got time to fortify, some to withdraw and some to change their tactics.

These defence tactics were not foolhardy. They actually brought a change in the Chinese attacks. It broke the Chinese advance. The Chinese thought it would be easy to walk all over the minuscule forward posts, but the tough fight given to them not only broke their advance, it lowered their spirits and broke their momentum. These were not fictional stories; they were true tales of courage and sacrifice. These soldiers were discovered like this much later, their positions telling the story of the war they had fought.

The story of the post of Sirijap 1 was told by Naik Rabilal Thapa and the surviving soldiers of various posts. It was fortunate that these episodes of bravery, great valour, and sacrifice could be told to the world. Otherwise, the stories, too, would have been buried with the soldiers.

In all probability, the outcome of this war would have been different if the Indian Air Force had been deployed. And there were many stories revolving around this theory. This has been addressed by Air Cmde (Retd) Ramesh Phadke in his article 'The Two Myths of 1962'.

The article spoke about General SPP Thorat's report about the eastern border of India. He was the General Officer Commanding-in-Chief of the Eastern Command of the Indian Army. He had done a thorough study of the eastern border and had realized that there were six passes through which large bodies of enemies could make inroads into India. Upon doing a survey of the area, he perceived that the landscape was easier for the Chinese troops to enter from their side of the border. It was less steep, and the landscape merged into the Tibetan plateau. However, these passes would become snow-bound during the winters, and the Chinese would have to go back since these routes would become difficult over a long period of time. To defend all of these points, Thorat wanted an in-depth position for his troops. He emphasized building proper roads on the Indian side to make travelling easy for their troops. He even enlisted additional troops and platoons, equipment, signals communication, mortars, and artillery needed to defend the eastern border.

A report regarding the same was sent to General Thimmaya, who further forwarded it to the then Defence Minister V.K. Menon. The latter didn't give much attention to the report, confident that his diplomatic skills would stop the Chinese from taking any such action. Therefore, the report never reached Nehru. This also became one of the reasons why the Indian Army was not as well prepared for the Chinese attack as it could have been.

Chapter 20

POW (Prisoner of War)

Jako rakhe saiyan maar sake na koi.

The doorbell rang and Shukla got up to open the door. She had been sitting and knitting a sweater for Dhan Singh. Having heard of stories of how cold it was in Chushul, she started to knit him a warm sweater. She left her knitting at the table and went to open the door. Seeing Manu and Bikram there surprised her. She was wondering how come they had not informed her that they were coming.

Draupadi had called them, after listening to the news from Chushul. She wanted them to be there with her and Shukla. After greeting them, she went and made some tea. It was nice to sit and chat with her brothers-in-law. They had always been loving and caring. After chatting for a while, they went off to rest.

Shukla while having tea, was trying to listen to the radio. Her two little girls were sitting next to her. The elder one Pamela, looking at the baby bump said, "Mine" while other one immediately put a hand on top of the stomach and said, "No, mine!"

"Shhhhhh!" said Shukla irritably.

She kept rotating the radio dial as she was unable to hear the news clearly. There was a lot of disturbance, and amidst all that crackling on the radio, she heard the news but did not understand it. The newsreader declared that Major Thapa had died in Sirijap after fighting valiantly. The newsreader was a Punjabi, and her accent was also Punjabi, so Shukla heard Major Dhyan Singh Thapa. Also, when Major Thapa left, he was a Captain, so she couldn't comprehend the implications of the news.

She commented to her mother-in-law, "Poor Major Thapa, he fought so bravely. His wife must be so miserable!"

Not for one minute did she think that that it was her husband, the newsreader was talking about. She called her two daughters and they sat in the temple room and like every evening they sat and sang, "*Tum hi ho mata, pita tum hi ho, tum hi ho bandhu, sakha tumhi ho.*" The prayer that meant God was their mother, their father, friend and everything, gave them solace.

Finishing their evening prayer, she hugged the girls. As always, she told them to pray for the safety of their father and the safety of all the soldiers out there fighting.

It was dinner time, and she went to the kitchen to get dinner ready for everybody. It was a strange evening. Everyone was very sober. Nobody was talking or even trying to talk. They were all looking down at their plates and trying to eat. It was like the calm before the storm. Generally, whenever Manu and Bikram came over, they would help her in the kitchen, and there would be such an uproar in the kitchen that she would shoo them out of her clean, rather pristine kitchen. Shukla was a compulsive cleaner. She maintained a sparkling house.

They would create chaos, playing pranks on everyone with the girls in tow. They would get up in the morning and the commotion would begin from then onwards.

But this time, everyone was quiet. Not a shout, nor a word

out of place from anyone. It was like everyone had this sixth sense which was telling them that something was wrong. No one was in any mood to do anything else, but listen to the news on the radio.

* * *

It was a bleak October day when Shukla had two officers from Major Dhan Singh's battalion visit her. She looked at them, looking at her sheepishly. They were in uniform, wearing a black arm band holding their caps, not knowing how to say what they had to say. They made her sit down and then broke the news to her. They told her that Major Dhan Singh had died fighting bravely in Sirijap and that the entire post had been wiped out. They narrated how bravely each and every soldier of that post had fought.

Shukla could never forget the horror of the seemingly peaceful afternoon. After hearing that terrible news, she began to wail in pain. Those wails could have broken anyone's heart into smithereens.

She did not cry. There were no tears. It was like she was in another world, and there was just this terrible howling that came from her chest, her eyes looking at everyone sightlessly. She could barely stand. Her legs refusing to take her weight buckled under her. Her daughters ran towards her, trying to hold her, but she kept pushing them away. The older daughter kept holding her as she collapsed on the floor. There were these horrible wails emitting from her body, petrifying the children. She kept saying, "Please don't tell me all these things. He will be back. He promised!"

Draupadi and Bikram picked her up and put her into bed. Draupadi cradled her like a little child and tried to soothe her, and she said, “It’s okay. It’s okay to cry. These are the ways of God. Be brave. Dhanu would want you to be brave. Think of your children. Think of the baby in your womb,” she said, forgetting her own loss.

“But he promised, Ma. He promised he would be back!” cried Shukla.

Pamela was wondering what was happening. Draupadi saw the confused look, she told her, “Go look after your sister.”

Pamela went away quietly. Madhulika was crying. She could sense that there was something amiss. Pamela was upset herself. She told the younger sister to keep quiet, but the younger one went on crying. Pamela gave her one tight slap. She then promptly hugged her in a tight embrace, clinging to each other as their tears mingled, trying to comfort each other in vain.

Pamela knew that her father had gone to war and something terrible had happened to him. After a while, she went to her grandmother and asked her, “What’s happening? Why is everyone crying?”

Draupadi hugged her tightly and said, “Your father has gone to God, and he is going to look after us from there.”

At that point, Pamela started crying, and there was no stopping her. She yelled, and she shrieked.

Shukla walked up to her, slapped her hard, and said, “He will be back!” she sternly declared. Then, she hugged her immediately.

Shukla couldn’t and wouldn’t believe the news. She kept saying, “This is not true; he told me he would be back. Yes, he said he would get me the highest gallantry award, but we were supposed to go and get it together."

She went to the temple and sat there with her daughters, clinging to her. She kept sitting there for hours till she was literally dragged out and fed some food. Draupadi made her lie down and sat with her, holding her hand.

It seemed like all the strength from this feisty old mother was gone. She had suddenly aged, and how! Her hands had shrivelled up, and there was no strength left in them. She could feel them trembling. The fingers had become nerveless, unable to hold anything, yet she tried. She knew Shukla wasn't in a state to do anything, so she had to make the effort. She had two small children to look after. She had Shukla to take care of and all the relatives to feed. After hearing the news, a stream of relatives had arrived to pay their condolences.

A letter of condolence stating Major Thapa's death from Lieutenant Colonel J.D. Karewal arrived on 27th October 1962, and another letter from General P.N. Thapar followed on 28th October 1962.

Har Bahadur Thapa, Shukla's father, arrived in Dehradun with her brother Shankar as soon as they received the terrible news.

But life goes on, and you can't help but follow the traditions that have been exercised over the years. Despite Shukla's convictions, the panditji was called the next day to perform the last rites of Major Thapa. Shukla was told to wear a white saree and sit in the puja ceremony. But she refused to wear white; she wore a light beige saree and kept reiterating throughout the puja, "Why are you doing this? He is going to be back!"

The panditji was very uncomfortable. He cleared his throat and told Shukla to sit down with him, looking at her sorrowfully.

Shukla sat on the carpet placed on the floor with great difficulty, her huge stomach making things more difficult. She was very uncomfortable as her back was troubling her.

They had a thirteen-day puja at home. The panditji was asked to come every day and perform the rituals for the deceased. Shukla was refusing to listen to anyone. The panditji kept insisting that she stop wearing coloured sarees and wear a white saree, but she refused.

Eventually, she had to give in to her mother-in-law. She started to wear beige-coloured sarees and no sindoor. Bindis and bangles were not allowed either. She was isolated from normal life during the ritual of cleansing or the *jhuto* period of death. She could not go out, nor could she visit the temple. She was forced to observe the traditional Hindu mourning period for thirteen days. After the death, during this time, the family is considered impure, and the members stay home.

The priest would come every day to lead the prayers and read the *Garuda Purana*. A big picture of Dhan Singh was placed in the prayer room, and a garland of flowers was put around the photo. A lamp was lit in front of the photo. For thirteen days, Shukla was not allowed to eat any kind of flavourful food.

She sat with the priest and listened to him chanting the prayers. Bikram would give the priest the prasad that was specially cooked for him. On the eleventh day, the havan was conducted. The last rites are known as *panchganga hom* where a mixture of cow's milk, dung, urine and ghee was sprinkled all over the house.

The thirteenth day was the final day of mourning. On this day, a community feast was organized for people staying in and around the house. There was a puja and havan and *pind sammelan*. This was a ritual performed to place the departed soul with the ancestors and god. On this day, alms were also given to the poor and to the priest, along with rituals to release the soul and support reincarnation.

Once the thirteen days were over, the panditji stopped coming. Her sister-in-law Shakuntala went back to Delhi to her family. Manu and Bikram left as well.

Shukla's solitary life began. She started praying a lot. Draupadi was trying her best to look after her. She would make sure that she would eat. Shukla had become careless about her meals. She just could not eat and hunger was the last thing on her mind. With great difficulty, she would swallow her food.

But Draupadi kept telling her, "You have to eat. You have to take care of the little baby inside you."

Listening to her mother-in-law's berating, she would try to eat. She felt bad for the brave old lady; she had lost a son, too, after all. The only earning son who had made something of himself. And now she had to take care of his wife and his children. But she was taking each day as it came. Shukla's father was still around, and so was Shankar.

Shukla's real mother was very religious. She had left her husband when her children were very young. But she had always remained in touch with her children. After she left her husband, she lived with different sects of religious people. As she grew older, for the longest time she lived in Sai Baba's ashram in Bangalore. When she learned of Dhan Singh's death, she asked Shukla to send the telegram to her.

She took the telegram announcing Dhan Singh's death to Chamundi Devi's mandir and prayed. She prayed to God that if the news in the telegram was not true, to let it fly away. She placed the telegram on the Goddess Chamundi Devi's feet. To her surprise, the telegram flew off from her feet onto the floor. Even though there had been no wind and nobody had entered or exited that room. It was a cave-like room, so it was quite uncanny that the telegram should fall from where it was placed. Radha, Shukla's mother, was so happy and so convinced that she had asked Shukla to stop all the death rites that were being performed at their house. But they were not stopped. According to Draupadi, all these rituals had to be performed for her son's soul's onward journey. This incident, though when related to Shukla, convinced her completely that her husband was alive.

He would come back. He had promised her.

***

Meanwhile, Major Thapa was taken to the Chinese army camp, where he was kept a prisoner. Nobody in the Indian side was aware of this. They had assumed he had perished. He was a prisoner of war for seven long months. He was mostly kept in solitary confinement. The Chinese were well known for their torturous interrogations. Major Thapa also had to undergo a series of interrogations and punishments.

One time, they forced him to remain awake for forty-eight hours at a stretch. They broke military conventions and inflicted inhumane punishments on Indian prisoners. Another day, he was told to trek across the frozen snow with no shoes and heavy radio equipment on his back. After walking the entire day, they allowed him to come back to his solitary cell in the evening.

Thapa sat down on the ground, cleaning his numb and bleeding feet with melted snow. Only if the Chinese knew that during his childhood, he had at times walked miles barefoot when his sandals had worn out! And he would be walking around with flapping sandals till some kind of donor donated a pair of shoes or sandals. Grimacing, he cleaned his feet, waiting for the next course of action the Chinese would take. He had heard the Chinese soldiers say that they were treating the Gorkha soldiers well, but he could not really trust the Chinese. They had entered his homeland and had attacked them all the while shouting, 'Hindi Chini, bhai bhai'.

And judging by the way he was being treated, it didn't seem like they were doing any better with the others. So, how could anyone trust them? They had troubled and harassed him a lot. They would ask for information from him, and when he refused to reply, they would threaten him and sometimes insult him. They had heard stories about him, about how he had killed a large number of their Chinese soldiers barehand with his khukri. There were many who had seen him fight and lead his men.

They would start questioning him and tell him that his government was not doing anything to release him and the three thousand other soldiers who had been taken prisoner of war by the Chinese. But he laughed at them, annoying them even more. Nothing scared Major Thapa any longer. He had danced with death and survived. He had seen his men embrace death with great valour. So, whatever the Chinese interrogators were doing was nothing in comparison.

He thought a lot about his men who died defending their land. He knew and much later understood the sentiments of Van Ekelen's *Indian Foreign Policy and the Border Dispute with China*, which was published later. In one of the book's chapters, it is said that it would have been wrong and repugnant to every sentiment of national honour and self-respect to acquiesce in aggression.

The prisoners at the Chinese camp here were quite underfed. They were given the same food for all their three meals. Then, there were prisoners who hadn't been allowed to have a bath for the entire duration of their confinement. Major Thapa used to take the frozen snow from the grounds outside, put it in a bucket, try to melt it and then clean himself with it.

Out of sheer habit he would pray every day. He had found a black oval stone with a half white circle at one end. He believed it to be a Shivling – a representation of lord Shiva. Every morning, he would pray to it, firmly believing it to be his Shiva.

One day, he was sitting and praying to his Shivling when one of the Chinese interrogators asked him, "Do you believe in God?"

Major Thapa replied, "Yes, I believe in God, and it is because of him I am sitting in front of you. Otherwise, I would have been dead during that attack of yours when it was raining bullets. It was a miracle that I survived. But when God saves you, nobody can kill you. *Jako rakhey Saiyan, maar sake na koi.*"

The Chinese took out his gun and said, "If I decide to kill you, how will your God save you?"

Major Thapa took off his jacket and replied with conviction, "Shoot and kill me if you can. But I didn't die when it was raining bullets. I survived, and if my God doesn't want me to die now, even if you do shoot me, I will survive!"

There was another soldier with Major Thapa in that prison at that moment. His name was Major Hasabnis from the 5 Jat regiment. He had been deployed near the Galwan river in Ladakh when he was taken prisoner.

He laughingly told Major Thapa, "Zip up your jacket, Thapa. You never know with these Chinese soldiers. If something clicks in his brain, he might really shoot you!"

But that was how a Gorkha soldier was: dauntless and daring.

The Chinese were nasty to the Indian prisoners. And especially towards Major Thapa, for he had not only inflicted a lot of damage on the Chinese but had also refused to make any statement against the Indian government. They could not break his spirit in spite of the terrible mental and physical torture they inflicted on him.

The Chinese, in one of their reports, had described the departure of the PoWs thus:

'The captured Indian officers and soldiers reluctantly bid farewell to the Chinese personnel, apparently not wanting to leave China... the Indian captives in farewell with the Chinese Red Cross staff cheered their arms: "Long live the friendship between the Chinese and Indian people!"'

The fact was that they had been chanting this even before the war, and they continued chanting this during the war and after the war was over. Who would ever trust the Chinese? They had given a new meaning to the word trust.

The Indo-China War of 1962 was one of the most unfortunate episodes of Indian history. It was a story of many untold deaths, many heroic performances, and a line of control washed red with the blood of our soldiers. But this war taught the nation many lessons, lessons for which the people and soldiers paid a heavy price.

According to James Calvin, India gained many benefits from the 1962 conflict. This war united the country as never before. India got 32,000 square miles (8.3 million hectares, 83,000 km2) of disputed territory even though she felt that NEFA had been hers all along. The new Indian republic had avoided international alignments; by asking for help during the war, India demonstrated its willingness to accept military aid from several sectors. And finally, India recognized the serious weaknesses in its Army. It would more than double its military manpower in the next two years, and it would work hard to resolve the military's training and logistic problems to later become the second-largest. India's efforts to improve its military posture significantly enhanced its Army's capabilities and preparedness.

This battle changed the course of the war of 1962. Because of the fierce fight they gave the enemy, the others got some time. Some could withdraw, while others were able to fortify. This wasn't just the charge of the light brigade – a brave but foolhardy charge. It actually brought about a strategic turnaround in the war of 1962 because it broke the Chinese advance and the momentum of the Chinese. It was also our good fortune that people survived, though just a handful of them, to tell us these stories, which would have been buried with the dead otherwise.

***

Major Dhan Singh Thapa prayed a lot. The prayers along with meditation had given him a lot of peace and an incredible strength of mind, which helped him deal with what came his way.

He befriended a small Chinese boy who used to bring them food. Major Thapa started to talk to him in sign language. The boy taught him to eat with chopsticks, and was very proud that he was teaching an officer how to eat with chopsticks. He became quite fond of Major Thapa who regaled him with stories of football and his family.

One day, he told this boy to post a letter for him. He wrote to his maternal uncle in Shimla, saying that he was alive and a prisoner of war. The letter reached Shimla on 30th December 1962.

On 4th January 1963 his brother-in-law Man Bahadur Thapa sent a letter to the Chief of Army Staff saying that a letter from Major Thapa had reached Shimla. And the letter said that he was alive and taken a prisoner of war. On the same day, Man Bahadur Thapa received confirmation from the government about the same information.

A letter from Colonel Tobit arrived.

> *Dear Mr Thapa,*
>
> *Please refer to your letter dated 4th January '63. I may inform you that your brother-in-law, Major D.S. Thapa, who was earlier reported killed, is reposted to be a prisoner of war with the Chinese.*

By 5th January 1963, the media had announced the news all over the country that Major Thapa was alive and a prisoner of war. Several efforts were being made by the Indian government to bring back their soldiers, and along with others, Major Thapa finally came back to his country after seven months.

When Shukla first heard the news, she was dumbfounded. Her husband was alive! She was elated that her faith in God was restored. Dhan Singh had got a second chance at life. They had got a second chance to be a family again. She became her old self again. She could not stop smiling and kept waiting for the bell to ring. Waiting to see Dhan Singh again, whom she thought she had lost forever.

And the bell did keep ringing, as there was a constant stream of friends and relatives coming over with their best wishes.

Every time the bell rang, Shukla's heart would start beating wildly. There was too much excitement in the house as Dhan Singh was expected home any moment. She dressed up in a pink saree and wore a pink bindi and her brand-new pink bangles. And while she was dressing up, she started to cry. This was the first time she cried, and she couldn't stop. Her daughters who were watching her getting dressed started to cry as well. Her mother-in-law came into the room to see what was wrong. She saw Shukla sitting in front of her dressing table with her bangles clasped in her hands and crying. Pamela was holding her from the back and Madhulika had her face on her mother's lap. Draupadi held all of them in a tight hug as they shed tears of joy together.

On 12th May 1963, the doorbell rang. Shukla just knew it was him. He returned to India on 10th May 1963 but reached Dehradun only after the military formalities were completed. Draupadi went to see who it was. She opened the door, and yes, there stood her son. Standing tall in front of her. Her joy knew no bounds. He touched her feet, and she blessed him. She was reminded of all the times when he had come and touched her feet on the football ground after he had scored a goal. He touched the priest's feet, who had approached behind her. They had called him specially to ask him to perform the rituals since his death rites had been conducted.

Panditji explained to the family that since the death rites had been performed, Shukla and Dhan Singh would have to get married again. There would be a proper prayer meeting and a havan. The wedding would be performed with complete rituals like before. Till then, Shukla and Dhan Singh could not meet each other. They would not be allowed to see each other. But Shukla would not hear of it. She was determined to see him with her own eyes. She wanted to see him and hear him that it was really him who had returned home.

She insisted so much that the panditji had to give in. He told her to get two-bed sheets – one for him and one for her. Both of them had to cover themselves with the sheets. Two holes were made on each sheet for only the eyes. They both donned the sheets and stood looking at each other. Shukla could not control herself. Tears falling, she asked him, "How are you?"

"I am good and in front of you because of you and my mother's prayers!" he replied.

Their two daughters were all over him. Nobody could stop the children from throwing themselves at Dhan Singh. He was like their prize trophy. They were hugging him and clinging on to him.

Pamela dragged him to the little baby's room to show him his son Paramdeep. Madhulika said with great pride, "Mine!"

She almost got one whack from Pamela, who did not put up with any kind of nonsense. This was their perpetual fight, but they kept quiet because they were too excited that their father was home.

Paramdeep was fast asleep. Dhan Singh picked up the little baby and hugged him close.

There was nothing more he wanted in life. After having done all he could for his country, to come back to his family and hug his newborn son was indeed God's blessing. A great sense of achievement hung around him like a warm, comfortable cloak.

He hugged the baby once again, taking in the euphoria. He handed the baby to Draupadi the minute the baby started crying. The baby could sense that there was a lot of excitement around him.

His grandmother Draupadi rocked him and he calmed down. He tried to keep his eyes open, but the rocking and the warmth of his grandmother's body were forcing the sandman to put him back to sleep. Draupadi gently put him in his cradle, putting two pillows beside him.

The girls came in running to ask their grandmother about their new clothes. She shushed them and gestured to them to go out. They refused to move till she wearily came out of the room to answer their queries.

"Where are our new clothes?" chorused the girls.

"We have been sent by Papa to get ready. I want to wear my new suit. My mummy and papa are getting married again, so I have to get ready and look very nice," said Pamela very seriously.

Shakuntala, their aunt, had managed to get some nice clothes for them. She took them to her room and helped them get ready. Madhulika and Pamela were thrilled to bits with their new finery and walked around like little princesses.

Dhan Singh went to see the arrangements being made for the wedding. Manu and Bikram were busy putting up the pyramidical Army tents that were being pitched outside the house for the prayers, havan and the wedding.

The little girls were wondering what was happening. Roaming in the garden, Madhulika climbed onto the tent and started sliding down. But the tent had only been half pitched; it collapsed with that brat on top of the heaped tent. She was sternly reprimanded and sent inside, and Draupadi told her to keep out of trouble. Giving her grandmother a loving hug, she ran inside to look for more mischief.

Draupadi, who had suddenly acquired Amazonian strength, got busy arranging everything. Her two other sons were given their duties, and they were more than happy to do so. For everyone, this was no less than a miracle, and everyone was in the mood to celebrate.

Draupadi asked, "Has all the work been delegated? Has the panditji got everything he needs? Otherwise, after every five minutes, you boys will run to get something!"

Manu replied, "Mataji, don't worry. Everything has been done."

"Where are the flowers?"

"Bikram has gone to get them."

"Is the puja thaali with the panditji?"

"Are you sure you have got dry sticks for the havan?"

So on and so forth it went on till finally everyone finally sat down for the puja.

Shukla insisted on wearing red. Dressed in a red saree, she and Dhan Singh got married for the second time. Shukla looked more beautiful than she had looked during her first marriage. With her red sindoor and her red bindi, she looked content. Happiness had given a breathtaking glow to her face. It was like a magic wand had been waved, and it had showered the whole household with euphoric bliss.

Pamela was wearing a red salwar suit with a golden dupatta. She had a gold tikka on her forehead and looked like a fragile doll. Madhulika wore a vibrant orange ghagra. Both of them sat with their father, both wearing very important looks on their faces and rubbing their eyes since the smoke from the havan was hurting their eyes. The priest performed the havan and the marriage ceremony with great elan. After some time, the excitement of sitting there listening to endless mantras fizzled off, and they started fidgeting. But one look from their grandmother made sure they both quietened down and kept sitting.

The couple took the pheras again. The bride walked behind the groom, and then it was time for the groom to walk behind the bride. The couple was now remarried. They walked to the panditji, touched his feet, and he very graciously blessed them. They then went to Draupadi, who hugged her son tightly and blessed him.

Now it was time for celebrations. A huge feast had been organized by the family. Dhan Singh's favourite dishes were made. In fact, there were more sweets than any other food as he had a huge sweet tooth. A huge broiler of kheer was made. He loved kheer, and if he had his way, he would have finished all of it. But his daughters could give him tough competition and they were also waiting for the dessert eagerly.

For Shukla, all this was like how she had imagined it to be – her husband sitting at the dining table eating his meal with them. His loud laughter resounded in the house ushering out the demons living in this house for the past few months.

***

On 2nd January 1963, Shukla gave birth to a baby boy, and they named him Paramdeep Thapa. The 'Param' was taken from the Param Vir Chakra. After all, that is what Dhan Singh had promised Shukla. And he had always kept his promises.

On 26th January 1964, Major Dhan Singh Thapa was honoured by the Param Vir Chakra medal.

The same year on 16th June, they were blessed with another baby girl who they called Poornima. For the longest time, she was teased by her other siblings, calling her a step-sister since she was born after the second wedding.

Poornima was the one who looked after Dhan Singh in his later years. His kidneys gave him trouble, but Poornima oversaw the dialysis at home every day. The daughter from their marriage after his return from China took over completely to take care of him. He died on 5th September 2005 in Pune of a heart attack.

***

After receiving the medal, Dhan Singh gave the medal to his wife Shukla and said, “Remember I promised you that I will get you the highest award so here it is. This one is especially for you!”

Shukla said, “I always knew that you’d come back and that you’d keep your promise and get me the highest gallantry award of the Indian Army.”

Like someone said, ‘*Legends are lessons; they ring with Truth.*’

Citation

Major Dhan Singh Thapa

1/8 Gorkha Rifles (IC 7990) Major Dhan Singh Thapa was in command of a forward post in Ladakh. On 20th October, it was attacked by the Chinese with overwhelming strength after being subjected to intensive artillery and mortar bombardment. Under his gallant command, the greatly out-numbered post repulsed the attack, inflicting heavy casualties on the aggressors. The enemy attacked again in greater numbers after heavy shelling by artillery and mortar fire. Under the leadership of Major Thapa, his men repulsed this attack, which also resulted in heavy losses to the enemy. The Chinese attacked for the third time with tanks to support their infantry. The post had already suffered large numbers of casualties in the earlier two attacks. Though considerably reduced in number, it held out to the last. When it was finally overrun by overwhelming numbers of the enemy, Major Thapa got out of his trench and killed several of the enemy in hand-to-hand fighting before he was finally overpowered by the Chinese soldiers.

Major Thapa's cool courage, conspicuous fighting qualities, and leadership were among the highest traditions of our army.

Gazette of India Notification

No. 68 -/62

My Dad, My Hero

He was a hero in the literal sense. Having been awarded the Param Vir Chakra, the highest gallantry award in India, he was actually a hero. And he was my hero!

He loved us, his children, unconditionally. His love was such a warm secure place to be in. His love for us was full of sacrifices. It was humbling and the most honest emotion in my life. All his life he faced difficulties, without letting us ever know. I guess most fathers do that – some more, some less.

Our childhood, thanks to him and my mother, was full of fun, full of love, full of happiness. His love, honesty, and bravery has made me what I am today. I would like to believe that I'm happy, honest and brave. It is his inheritance to us.

Dad, you gave us beautiful memories. How can I forget those fun-filled afternoons trying to make ice cream in that cranky wooden ice cream maker, cranking it up for hours, or those evenings when we gorged on jalebis and samosas, and those holidays which started and ended with our sojourn with God and his temples. Those joyous festive evenings when we sang our prayers and did not remember the lyrics; how we would giggle endlessly. We lacked nothing emotionally and materialistically. I thank God for my wonderful dad.

Thank you, Dad, for being my dad. And thank you, God, for my dad.

Madhulika Thapa Monga (Daughter)

He was a wonderful person and a great father-in-law. We got along very well. I remember very fondly of the time spent together during our Dussehra get-togethers. He was a man who gave no advice, which according to me, was an acceptance of one and all as they were. I pray to God for him to be at peace.

Amaan Monga (Son-in-Law)

My dearest dad was an adorable father and an awesome human being. He was the bravest of the brave. A great warrior who defended his motherland by fighting a most ferocious battle in a difficult terrain.

He was always cheerful against all odds. He always encouraged us to enjoy life but gave equal importance to education. He believed in gender equality and gave his daughters and his son equal opportunities. He was religious and at the same time, liberal. We are all married into different communities, and he never raised any objection. All these qualities have been inculcated in us, and I am extremely proud to be his oldest daughter. Of not only a braveheart but also an extremely humble human being. Please, Dad, bless us so that we can always tread on the path you have shown us. Love you, Dad.

Pamela Thapa Chauhan (Oldest Daughter)

My father-in-law was the simplest of human beings. A great soldier who fought valiantly to defend our motherland. We are all very proud of you. Please shower your blessings on all of us.

Lt. Col. Ranbir Chauhan (Oldest Son-in-Law)

Dad was a very simple person. A very simple soul. I remember when I was seven years old, I got caught stealing money from my mother's cupboard. I thought he would skin me alive. But surprisingly, he sat me down, and made me understand what I had done wrong. A thorough gentleman who would explain things so beautifully that no one could forget those conversations. Another very important thing about him was that he was a very positive man. I never heard anything negative from him.

Lt. Col. Paramdeep Thapa (Son)

I don't remember my dad ever preaching to me about anything. I learnt everything from his actions. He led by example. Since childhood, I saw how he treated the people working for him and how he respected them and valued their time and effort. He was mostly jovial and cheerful. He never burdened us with his financial or health problems but, by example, made us value money and food as sacred, ours and others. He made us tough to withstand all the storms of life. I remember his thumbs-up sign and saying 'fit and fine' whenever anyone asked him how he was during the days when his kidneys had started to fail. The best lesson I learned from him again, by example, was to enjoy life in all weather, literally and figuratively. To enjoy simple things in life and to create maximum happiness with minimal resources. Another valuable lesson I learned from him was to always participate in others' happiness and be a moral support in times of sadness for others. In fact, the day he nearly fainted and was diagnosed with kidney failure, he had been attending someone's funeral.

I have such happy memories of our childhood that included numerous picnics and train journeys. Everything was budgeted, but happiness was unlimited. His coming on leave when he was on the field was such a treat for us. We would be so happy to have him with us, and he would indulge us without compromising our discipline. Once I remember going for a walk with him and buying ice cream from a cycling ice cream man. We had walked a bit ahead when I realized that the ice cream man had given 50 paise extra change. My father made me run behind that ice cream man to return the money. Whatever compassion, values, and high fun quotient I have are all thanks to my father.

And lastly, I remember the beautiful smile he gave me before passing away to a better place. Even to his death, he went smiling. That was the stuff my father was made of. To me, he was the best father, I could have wished for no other.

Poornima Thapa (Third Daughter)

Dad was brave, charismatic, and a deeply family-oriented person. A true hero not only on the battlefield but also in the hearts of those who knew him. Salute him always.

Anushree Thapa, (Daughter-in-Law)

Nana was someone whom we have always looked up to and felt very proud of. His courage and stories have always intrigued us and made us respect and honour him greatly. He was a great man who loved his family and his nation. He was a true inspiration, and we hope we can make him proud too.

Geetanjli Chauhan (Granddaughter)

Nana's Gorkha courage was legendary, but it was his kindness that left the biggest impression on my heart. He taught me the value of family and showed me that love can conquer even the toughest of challenges. To me, he will always be a hero in every sense of the word.

Sanyukta Chauhan (Granddaughter)

I am incredibly proud to be the granddaughter of a Param Vir Chakra awardee, a hero whose bravery and sacrifices inspire me every day. Living in London, I often share his stories with great passion, hoping to inspire others with his extraordinary courage and selflessness. His life was a testament to the highest ideals of service, resilience, and love for one's country. Among the many lessons he imparted, one that stands out is resilience and bravery - a principle that has shaped my own approach to life and work. I'm so proud of him and remain deeply inspired by his courage. His memory is a constant source of strength and pride, and I will forever cherish and honour the legacy he has left behind.

Subhadra Monga (Granddaughter)

Aayo Gorkhali! Will always remember you for your wit, humour, passion and dedication to your own.

Aneesha Thapa (Granddaughter)

He will forever be remembered as our hero. His zest for everything in life motivates us to push ourselves to new heights and excel in all our endeavours. We salute this fearless Gorkha and our beloved grandfather with deep admiration and gratitude.

Sean Thapa (Grandson)